TREASURES
OF THE NATIONAL TRUST

TREASURES

OF THE NATIONAL TRUST

EDITED BY ROBIN FEDDEN
ASSOCIATE EDITOR: ROSEMARY JOEKES

BOOK CLUB ASSOCIATES
LONDON

THIS EDITION PUBLISHED 1976 BY
BOOK CLUB ASSOCIATES

BY ARRANGEMENT WITH JONATHAN CAPE LTD
© 1976 BY THE NATIONAL TRUST

PRINTED IN GREAT BRITAIN BY
BUTLER & TANNER LTD, FROME AND LONDON

Contents

Acknowledgments

The National Trust makes grateful acknowledgment to the Director of the Victoria and Albert Museum for permission to include works of art at Ham House and Osterley Park, and textiles on loan from the Museum to Montacute and Oxburgh; to Sir John Carew-Pole Bt., the Trustees of the Faringdon Collection, and Lord St Oswald, for permission to include works of art from the collections wholly in their ownership at Antony House, Buscot, and Nostell Priory; to Lord Egremont, Sir Edmund Fairfax-Lucy Bt., Sir Richard Hyde Parker Bt., and Lord Sackville for permission to include certain works of art on loan to the Trust at Petworth, Charlecote, Melford, and Knole; to Major J. G. B. Chester for permission to include furniture on loan at Montacute. The National Trust much appreciates the courtesy and co-operation of these owners and of the Victoria and Albert Museum.

The National Trust also gratefully acknowledges the permission of the Waddesdon Trustees to reproduce illustrations from the folio catalogues to the Waddesdon Collection.

Illustrations

The editors and publishers are grateful to the following for permission to reproduce photographs: Olive Cook (for the late Edwin Smith), for pl. 64; A. F. Kersting, for pls. 67, 91, 95; the Victoria and Albert Museum, for pls. 10, 35, 52, 53, 55, 61, 62, 75, 102, 159; the Trustees of the Waddesdon Collection, for pls. 13, 15, 24, 43, 47, 86, 88, 105, 106, 108, 110, 130, 131, 142, 146; Jeremy Whitaker, for pls. 33, 71, 77, 100, 101

All other photographs have been commissioned for or taken from the National Trust Photographic Library.
Photographers:
John Bethell: 1, 2, 5, 7, 8, 12, 14, 19, 21, 22, 32, 34, 36, 37, 39, 41, 44, 45, 49,

ACKNOWLEDGMENTS

51, 52, 56, 57, 58, 60, 63, 66, 70, 72, 73, 74, 78, 79, 80, 84, 85, 87, 92, 97, 99, 103, 107, 109, 111, 118, 121, 123, 124, 125, 129, 133, 134, 135, 136, 137, 139, 141, 143, 145, 147, 148, 153, 154, 157, 158, 160, 162, 164, 165, 167, 168, 170
Blinkhorns: 119
Robert Chapman Photography: 96, 113, 117, 122, 128, 138
A. C. Cooper Ltd: 11, 31, 38, 90, 98, 140, 151, 156, 161, 163, 169
Courtauld Institute, University of London: 16, 17, 18, 23, 25
J. R. Freeman Ltd: 94
Christopher Hanson-Smith: 144
Angelo Hornak: 65, 69, 114, 116, 120
Eric de Maré: 54
National Trust: 3, 4, 27, 50, 59, 68, 81, 83, 89
Stephanie van Piere: 76
Jeremy Whitaker: 6, 9, 20, 26, 29, 30, 40, 42, 46, 48, 82, 93, 104, 112, 115, 126, 127, 150, 152, 155, 166
Andy Williams: 28

Foreword

by the Earl of Antrim, Chairman of the National Trust

Treasures of the National Trust is a logical complement to *The National Trust Guide* which appeared in 1973. The latter described the properties that the Trust owns and conveyed a clear idea of the diversity of its responsibilities. This new publication is an introduction to its collections, and reveals the aesthetic importance, and the rarity, of much of the furniture, porcelain, silver, and other objects in its care.

The Europalia Exhibition of works of art from Trust houses, organized in Brussels two years ago jointly with the National Trust for Scotland, demonstrated for the first time the range and quality of our collections. But it also clearly indicated the need for a survey in book form, such as *Treasures of the National Trust* provides. I hope this scholarly volume will make many of our splendid possessions more familiar to members and the general public.

Map showing principal collections

Wallington

Castlecoole

Sizergh Castle

Beningbrough Hall • Treasurer's
House

Nostell Priory

Manchester

Tatton Park

Lyme Park

Penrhyn
Castle

Little Moreton • Hardwick Hall
Hall

Erddig •

Sudbury Hall

Shugborough

Attingham

Powis Castle

Wightwick
Manor

Birmingham

Felbrigg
Hall

Blickling

Oxburgh Hall

Packwood

Coughton Court •

Charlecote Park

Upton House •

Anglesey Abbey

Ickworth

Melford Hall

Waddesdon Manor •

Ascott

Buscot •

West Wycombe
Fenton Hse.

Dyrham Park

Osterley

Ham Hse.

Clevedon
Court

Lacock

London

Arlington
Court

Stourhead •

Montacute •

The Vyne

Clandon
House

Polesden
Lacey

Knole

Scotney
Castle Gdns

Petworth

Uppark

Handcross

St Michael's
Mt.

Lanhydrock

Cotehele

Saltram

Antony House

I

Introduction

Robin Fedden

The modest buildings that came to the National Trust in its early days were unfurnished. Most of them dated from the Middle Ages or Tudor times. A fourteenth-century parish priest's house at Alfriston in Sussex, and a chantry chapel with a fine Norman doorway at Buckingham, were characteristic acquisitions. It was not until the Trust had been in existence for forty-five years that the contents of a great country house came into its ownership with the munificent bequest of Blickling from Lord Lothian in 1940.

Both Lord Lothian's example, and the penal taxation that has proved so great a threat to country houses, led to the subsequent acquisition of other outstanding collections. Many came as splendid and generous gifts: for example the collections at Waddesdon, Wallington, Ascott, Upton, Stourhead, and Sizergh. Such gifts, made sometimes at considerable sacrifice, secured for the nation works of art of inestimable value. Since 1953 when the Treasury was empowered to accept, and transfer to the Trust, works of art offered in satisfaction of estate duty, other collections of the first importance—such as Ickworth with its superb eighteenth-century silver, Petworth with its Turners and classical marbles, Hardwick with its unique assembly of tapestries and needlework—have come to the Trust through the sympathetic co-operation of the Government.

Today about sixty National Trust houses contain collections of consequence. Sometimes the chief interest of these collections is historic rather than artistic. Reflecting with exceptional fidelity the life and outlook of successive generations, they represent the deposit of many tides of taste, tides which were once impelled by the great moons of social, political, and economic change. Though lying deep in the countryside, a Wallington or a Melford echoes the reverberations of high policy, the clamour of faction, and the march of armies. The foundation of the Levant Company in the late sixteenth century brought oriental carpets and 'Rhodian' ware; with the return of Charles II from the Low Countries came the Dutch marquetry; the revocation of the Edict of Nantes filled state rooms with the craftsmanship of Huguenot immigrants;

oriental porcelain arrived as a by-product of the trading policy of the East India Company; the Peace of Paris in 1763, which enabled Englishmen to set out again on the Grand Tour, resulted in shipments of the latest wares from France and Italy; the huge sales that followed the French Revolution brought the sumptuous works of the finest *ébénistes*; Napoleon's Egyptian campaign introduced motifs from the Nile and ormolu sphinxes.

While such great houses reflect European history, those of the yeomanry, of which so few regrettably have preserved their contents, speak engagingly of local customs and crafts. At this modest level, Townend in the Lake District is among the most historically informative of the Trust's houses. Here, independent and intelligent, the Browne family lived for nearly three hundred years. The contents of their unpretentious house provide an extraordinary, perhaps a unique, insight into a particular way of life (pl. 68). There are eighteenth-century fabrics woven in cottages near by that reflect ancient Scandinavian influence; the furniture, barely alluding to the feverish changes of taste that affected great houses, was made by local craftsmen or by the Brownes themselves; the paintings of livestock are by Lakeland journeymen whose names are unfamiliar to the art market; and not least there is a little library which reveals the wide and humane preoccupations of a class that has almost vanished. While the contents of a Townend are rarely works of art, they indicate the variety of historical and social reference that lends interest to so many Trust interiors.

It is not however with the overtones of history, or with family associations, that *Treasures of the National Trust* is concerned. The chapters that follow have a different purpose. They select categories of furnishings in Trust houses—pictures, sculpture, tapestries, English and French furniture, European and oriental ceramics, and silver—and within these categories isolate objects which we have come to regard as works of art in their own right, or as worthy of special notice on account of their rarity or antiquity. Apart from an exhibition, arranged in conjunction with the Scottish National Trust, at the Palais des Beaux Arts in Brussels in 1973, this is the first time that so wide a range of works of art in Trust houses has been presented for special consideration.

No doubt this artistic and antiquarian approach, characteristic of our time, would have surprised many of those for whom these works of art were made. Until some hundred years ago there was a preference for the contemporary. It is well to recall that the contents of most seventeenth- and eighteenth century houses were *new* when acquired. Though a few antiquarians filled their 'cabinets' with the wrack of past centuries, and classical antiquities were prized for their rarity and associations, the modern obsession with the antique was foreign to our ancestors. Age did not generally confer distinction; if anything the reverse was true. Old furniture, unless cherished for particular dynastic reasons, was furniture ripe for replacement. The same applied to old tapestries and china. The most precious finds have thus often been made in the Trust's attics and servants' bedrooms; and when sixteenth- and seventeenth-century furniture has survived in state apartments, as at Hardwick or Knole, special circumstances usually account for its presence. At Hardwick such furniture was preserved because, with the building of Chatsworth only a few miles away, the house became largely redundant before the end of the seventeenth century: the Cavendishes did not think the contents of a mansion used for brief visits, or as a dower house, were worth keeping up-to-date. At Knole it was probably the vast size of the place that saved the old furniture. Following the replacement of retainers by paid servants, and a steep rise in prices in the second half of the sixteenth century, the house was an expensive burden by Charles I's time. Whereas in the family apartments furniture was replaced as taste changed (oak, ebonized pieces, walnut, mahogany, satinwood and rosewood, following in due sequence), expense fortunately prohibited the replacement of the old-fashioned furniture in the silent apartments and long, draughty galleries that looked on empty courtyards. At Uppark, to take another example, the splendid furnishings of the second half of the eighteenth century were preserved intact only by the piety of Sir Harry Fetherstonhaugh's young wife and younger sister-in-law who maintained Sir Harry's rooms unchanged until the second half of the nineteenth century. By that time the attitude to the furnishings of the past had decisively altered; their very age ensured their further retention.

As *Treasures of the National Trust* clearly indicates, country-house owners of the seventeenth and eighteenth centuries were intent on keeping abreast of the newest developments. No doubt in doing so they wished to impress their neighbours; but if they bought for prestige, they did not, as so many do now, buy with an eye to appreciation. In a day when there was a restricted market for anything but the up-to-date, their acquisitions — the lacquer cabinets, the Mortlake tapestries, the walnut settees, the Kent consoles, the portraits and the sporting pictures — must often have lost value almost as soon as they were installed. But if these owners were not historically minded, they had an eye for design and quality. Above all, they were concerned with craftsmanship. The concept of an art impervious to time, and of the role that inspired genius may play in its production, was not commonly present to their minds. Unbewitched by the magic of autograph works, these owners realized that good painters sometimes produce bad pictures. They often preferred a faithful copy of a compelling composition to a lesser but original work by the same master. Unterrorized by art historians, they took pleasure in competent studio works, and regarded pictures primarily as decoration for their walls. It reflects the prevailing attitude that in the seventeenth and eighteenth centuries fine furniture and tapestries, the products of exact and laborious craftsmanship, usually cost more than paintings.

This attitude to furnishing was one of many things that drastically changed about the middle of the nineteenth century. The era of the collector arrived, and a sense of history began to dominate furnishing. Age in itself conveyed prestige. Country gentlemen no longer showed a preference for the contemporary. In houses owned by the Trust, this change is perhaps first noticeable at Speke, substantially refurnished in a 'Jacobean' manner in the middle of the century, and at Charlecote. But it is the collections dating from the late nineteenth and twentieth centuries—notably Waddesdon, Polesden Lacey, Ascott, Upton and Anglesey Abbey—that fully reflect a revolution in taste and outlook. The impact of such houses, splendid though they may be, is very different from that of a Saltram or a Petworth which represents a slower organic growth. In the imposing new collections, the oriental carpets were not ordered through the factors of the Levant Company, the armorial porcelain was not commissioned from the potters of Kiangsi, the rococo mirrors were not specially designed for the house by Lock or Chippendale, and the rosewood bookcases did not come direct from Gillow; such things were assembled, often with fine discrimination, at auctions and from antique dealers. The results can be dazzling, but the reverberations of history, the murmur of the tides of taste, are muted.

While indicating the rich material in the Trust's houses generally, *Treasures of the National Trust* reveals that, in the context of such a book, these late nine-teenth- and twentieth-century collections have special importance. This is not surprising. They were assemblages of the splendid and the rare; the works of art cover a long time-span. In the eighteenth century no one would have acquired Quattrocento paintings, such as those at Upton and Polesden Lacey, or the wares of the Sung dynasty, so well represented at Ascott. On the other hand the older collections emphasize the generous and eclectic taste exercised by the earlier country-house owner in his choice of contemporary furnishings. From the time that Bess of Hardwick bought French pieces for her great Derbyshire house, the Continent was recurrently laid under tribute. Yet works of native inspiration held their own with the artistic productions of Europe and the East. Moreover, as will be evident from the illustrations to this book, they usually bore a stamp that set them clearly apart from the wares that travelled across the Channel. Even after the Restoration, when continental influence was at its height, our own production remained rich and varied. English craftsman-ship has perhaps never been more imaginative than at the turn of the century. The carving of Grinling Gibbons and his school—to be seen at Petworth, Sudbury, and other Trust houses—attained an astonishing virtuosity; the silver was superb, clockmakers—Quare, Tompion, and many more—were hardly rivalled; the new factory at Soho was turning out tapestries of wonder-ful colour and fantasy; furniture was daringly rich and elaborate.

The illustrations to *Treasures of the National Trust* also emphasize how much furnishings in every century owed to architecture, the master art. In these pages the contents of state rooms repeatedly take up themes first elaborated in stone.

Buildings such as Miller's Gothick hall at Lacock eventually inspire the ogival decoration of coal-scuttles. With the Hardwick gaming-table (pl. 69) the architectural influence of the Renaissance comes to sixteenth-century Derbyshire; objects as different as the Dyrham bookcase (pl. 76) and the silver wine-cooler by Robert Cooper (pl. 153) reflect the building vocabulary of the late seventeenth century; the furnishings at Rievaulx (pl. 73) speak of Palladio; and the motifs of neo-classical architecture find comfortable expression in a Queensborough tureen or a library table (pl. 99).

Treasures of the National Trust also reveals, not surprisingly, certain lacunae. The Trust, unlike a museum, can rarely acquire works of art to 'fill gaps'. Apart from a few relatively modern collections in its ownership, it conserves the often haphazard accumulations of successive generations. As already indicated, these derive a special interest from their presentation in their original setting. But the Trust's situation, while illustrating the force of La Bruyère's dictum, 'Les belles choses le sont moins hors de leur place', inevitably means that the contents of its houses cannot always illustrate the orderly development of a particular art-form. Thus the Trust has inherited no outstanding early eighteenth-century collection of paintings comprising, as such collections often did, large baroque and classical works. Similarly, though late seventeenth- and eighteenth-century English furniture is well represented, there are (apart from the examples of Thomas Hope's furniture at Buscot) few exceptional pieces of the Regency period.

The conservation of the many collections which provide the matter for this book raises continuing problems. In dealing with them the Trust is advised by an Arts Panel of experts distinguished in a variety of fields. However the virtual disappearance of certain types of craftsmen causes growing concern. While there is no shortage of good cabinet-makers, men competent to deal with the repair of lacquer, boulle, and in particular the painted furniture of the late eighteenth century, can be found only with difficulty. The problems of conservation are further intensified by the fact that the experienced housekeeper, who was once charged with the care of every great house, now rarely exists. The same is true of the able needlewomen on whom she could call. Further, the textiles for which they were responsible are now more often subject to the damaging effects of light than they were in the past. Most state apartments, with their embroidered seat furniture, their tapestries, their cut Genoa velvets and their Spitalfields silks, were once shuttered or curtained when not in use. Now that they have been thrown open to visitors, many have been exposed to more sunlight in a decade than in the preceding century. In the circumstances the repair of textiles has become urgent, and the Trust has recently established a textile workshop at Knole to overcome the grave shortage of trained needlewomen. It proposes to set up others. At the same time, windows have been treated at certain properties to exclude ultra-violet rays, and at houses like

Hardwick, where there are textiles of outstanding importance, special curtains have been fitted that can remain drawn even on visiting days.

Such measures illustrate, in the field of textiles, the positive curatorship which the Trust exercises. The care of other works of art, such as paintings or furniture, poses different but no less immediate issues. Since the Trust has become responsible for furnishings which rival those of the largest museums, it has perforce adopted something of a museum approach to conservation. It is convinced that such an approach can be perfectly compatible with the 'lived in' atmosphere which so greatly contributes to the charm of many of the Trust's houses.

2

Paintings

Denys Sutton

The paintings and drawings that greet visitors when wandering round the properties of the National Trust in many different parts of the country are extraordinarily varied and contain examples of the main European schools. The Trust's possessions constitute, in fact, a vast private collection that has been assembled, not by one person but by a varied range of patrons who bought what took their fancy and never bothered about such modern concepts as 'filling gaps'. The result provides, as it were, a tribute to the eclecticism of generations of private buyers and, in the aggregate, the Trust's pictures afford a bird's-eye view of English taste from the sixteenth and seventeenth centuries onwards.

This assemblage may be approached in a variety of ways—aesthetic, historical and sociological. In looking at such paintings, one may speculate about the personalities of the former owners. What induced them to acquire one painting in preference to another, where did they buy it and what did they pay for it? Fortunately, the careful cataloguing of the collection by the Trust's Adviser on Paintings often provides the answers to such questions.

While Ascott, Upton, Waddesdon, Petworth and Stourhead, to mention only five collections, are picture galleries in their own right, some houses are distinguished for isolated works of importance or paintings that are of historic rather than aesthetic significance. But it is unusual to come across a house which does not contain something to catch the eye. How typical it is of the unexpected treasures that belong to the Trust to find in the Bearsted collection at Upton a rare example of French medieval art, nothing less than a vivid miniature of *St Michael Slaying the Dragon* (pl. 1), from the celebrated Book of Hours illuminated by Jean Fouquet, for Étienne Chevalier, between 1452 and 1460, of which most of the other leaves are in the Musée Condé at Chantilly.

Although English collectors were among the first to appreciate early Italian art when William Roscoe (whose pictures are now in the Walker Art Gallery, Liverpool) gave the lead, few important works from this period belong to the Trust. This is mainly due to the fact that many of the collections in the Trust's

B

possession were formed in the seventeenth or eighteenth centuries, by men such as the Earl-Bishop of Derry at Ickworth. However, two collections assembled in more recent times at Upton and Polesden Lacey, by Viscount Bearsted and Mrs Ronald Greville, a famous hostess, possess examples of fifteenth-century Italian art.

The gem is undoubtedly Giovanni di Paolo's *The Presentation of the Virgin* (pl. 7) at Upton. This was once in the collection of Mrs Otto Kahn, whose husband was a prominent New York financier and one of the founders of the Metropolitan Opera. How interesting to think that this exquisite painting hung in his handsome Renaissance-style *palazzo*, a few blocks beyond the Metropolitan Museum! This enchanting Sienese painting, which dates from *c.* 1445–1450, is part of a predella, but the other panels are now lost. Giovanni di Paolo gave his pictures the allure of a precious object and, in this case, the blues, reds and golds endow this small masterpiece—it measures some eight inches by ten—with luxurious appeal. Giovanni's feeling for elegance led him to introduce into the composition two fashionable ladies whose presence helps to explain the popularity enjoyed by Sienese Quattrocento art at the end of the nineteenth century.

In our time much is made of the need for an artist to demonstrate originality at all costs, but art historians are aware that for many earlier painters dependence on the past was only natural (a case in point is Rubens, who did not hesitate to borrow heavily from his predecessors). In *The Presentation of the Virgin* Giovanni di Paolo's two attendant figures derive from the left side of Gentile de Fabriano's painting of the same subject in the Louvre. Echoes of a picture of *c.* 1425 in the Vatican Gallery by a master called the Pseudo-Pellegrini di Mariano and of Lorenzetti's fresco in the church of San Leonardo al Lago, near Siena, may also be observed: the former offers a precedent for the architecture, the latter for the group of onlookers. Such connections stress the sense of continuity that is such a feature of Italian art.

Twenty years or so before Giovanni di Paolo's death, the Flemish master, Roger van der Weyden, painted the tender portrait of an unknown man (pl. 2), also in the Bearsted collection, the background of which has been painted over. Its function is not altogether clear. It would be tempting to think that it was conceived as the portrait of a donor for the wing of a devotional diptych, but Professor Panofsky suggested that it may have been cut out of a larger composition. The question of its origin does not detract from the quality as a portrait, and it possesses unity of form as of feeling. Roger's gift for endowing his portraits with verisimilitude is particularly evident in the articulation of the hands, which have the look, and almost the feel, of a medieval ivory; they add to the mood of piety which infuses the portrait.

This picture is one of the many works from this period that brings up the vital question of the relationship between painting and sculpture in Flanders, a subject that has never been treated with the attention it deserves. Why was it that fifteenth-century Flemish masters were able to make their figures look as if they were carved out of stone or wood? Their depiction of architectural or sculptural detail is meticulous and figures are often painted in grisaille on the back of triptychs in imitation of sculpture.

One Fleming with a special talent for grisaille was Pieter Brueghel the Elder, the subject-matter of whose paintings sometimes distracts attention from the refinement of his technique. Although some authorities have questioned the authenticity of the grisaille, *The Dormition of the Virgin* (pl. 3), another Upton picture, only this master could have produced such a vigorous and effective painting. The argument that the fault of perspective detected under the chair is unworthy of the master is not acceptable: this detail shows the free handling of a work designed as the model for an engraving, published in 1574.

The special flavour of the picture, the interpretation of which has stimulated considerable discussion, derives from its being a night scene—a difficult subject for any artist, but one which Brueghel successfully tackled. Prototypes for the composition exist: a miniature, *La Mort,* from the *Grimani Breviary* and Schongauer's famous engraving, *The Death of the Virgin.* These are digested by the artist into a work in which the sorrowful nature of the event is heightened, not diminished, by such telling details as the figure of St John, who has fallen asleep from exhaustion at this critical moment. How brilliantly the artist has rendered the features of the Virgin, whose pallor announces her death, and the crowd standing at the door. *The Dormition,* like many other pictures in the Trust's collections, has an intriguing history. It possibly belonged to the famous geographer Abraham Ortelius, who commissioned the engraving, and it was probably owned by Rubens. This is hardly surprising, for it is just the sort of painting that appealed to him and influenced his style.

Another Renaissance painting, this time Italian, with an interesting history is Andrea del Sarto's *The Madonna and Child with St John* (pl. 4), *c.* 1521. This was acquired in Italy by Count Josef Fries, who spent two years from 1785 to 1787 there, where he met Goethe, who wrote in a letter that the Count had paid 600 zecchini for the painting and that the painter Angelica Kauffmann regretted that she did not buy it when she had the chance. It was purchased from the Count by the third Marquess of Londonderry then Lord Stewart, the British Ambassador from 1814–22 in Vienna (where he enjoyed a notorious love affair with Wilhelmina, Duchess of Sagan). The painting remained with his descendants until 1870, when it was purchased by Baron Lionel de Rothschild; it is now at Ascott.

Only since its cleaning have its full charms and lively colour emerged, and proof of its authenticity: *pentimenti* appear, notably in the Christ Child's leg and in the contours of His face. Its originality may be also observed, to quote St John Gore, 'in unfinished or suggested passages of painting—e.g. the hand and mouth of the Child and the fingers of St John'. Now Goethe's comment that it was 'an unbelievably beautiful picture' can be seen to be justified, at any rate in terms of Sarto's *œuvre*.

The vagaries of taste are ever fascinating. How illuminating of artistic appreciation in the 1890s that Berenson devoted his first book (1895) to Lorenzo Lotto, whom he interpreted as a 'psychological painter'! When this volume was published, the *Portrait of a Prelate* (pl. 5), *c.* 1505 (also at Ascott), was unknown; it turned up in the collection of Achillito Chiesa in Milan. At that time the picture was attributed to Alvise Vivarini, a painter whose use of tonal modulations and clarity of expression owed much to Antonello da Messina. Vivarini's influence is discernible in this painting, which, early in date, may be related to the *Portrait of Bernardo de' Rossi* of 1505, in the Capodimonte Gallery at Naples, and to a black chalk drawing in the Albertina, Vienna.

The rapid changes that can occur in outlook among artists of a specific school emerge when the Ascott Lotto is compared with *The Man in a Plumed Hat* (pl. 6) by Titian at Petworth, a picture which was probably painted some ten years later. When it entered the collection at Petworth House is not known, but how tempting to think that it came from the Northumberlands; if it did, its acquisition would have been in keeping with the taste of Charles I and the Earl of Arundel, who entertained such an affection for Venetian art of the Cinquecento.

Titian is a tantalizing painter. He could paint scenes of violence (as in the fresco at Padua, which Degas copied), or profound religious scenes; as a portraitist he had sharp insight—the self-portrait at Berlin for instance—but he could also sound a poetical note. The Petworth portrait owes something to the dreamy nostalgia and romantic world of Giorgione, and it may be related to *The Concert,* now given to Titian, in the Palazzo Pitti. It has, too, some of the enigmatic character of Giorgione's art. Who is this sitter? Is he a lover who has written a sonnet to his *inamorata*? Or does the sitter represent Giorgione, as has been claimed? One difference between Giorgione and Titian is made clear in this portrait by the latter's painterly treatment of the feather on the hat and his placing of the figure in space. Yet both artists shared a liking for portraying the psychological stress which, in Venetian art, forms a foil to the more extrovert panache of the tradition of pageant-painting that runs from Carpaccio through Veronese to Canaletto and Guardi. And Titian's portrait is a distant and more aristocratic ancestor of the *bravi* of Caravaggio and his followers.

Venetian influence occurs in one of the most dazzling paintings in the Trust's possession—El Greco's *El Espolio* (pl. 14) at Upton. After leaving his native Crete this artist spent some time in Venice, where the brilliant portrait style he developed owed something to Tintoretto, whose influence is reflected in the man in armour to the left of Christ. Some of the heads, too, recall Bassano. But the Venetian current was not the only one to fire El Greco's imagination: the

1 Jean Fouquet (*c.* 1420–*c.* 1481)   *St Michael Slaying the Dragon*   vellum $6\frac{1}{8} \times 4\frac{5}{8}$ in.
Upton House

2 Roger van der Weyden (*c.* 1399–1464)
   Unknown Man   panel 7 × 6 in.
   Upton House

3 Pieter Brueghel the Elder (active 1551–69)
   The Dormition of the Virgin (detail)
   panel 14½ × 21 in.
   Upton House

4 Andrea del Sarto (1486–1531)   *Madonna and Child with St John*   panel 40 × 29½ in.   Ascott

5 Lorenzo Lotto (*c.* 1480–1556)
A Prelate   canvas 17¾ × 14¼ in.
Ascott

6 Titian (*c.* 1487/90–1576)
Man in a Plumed Hat
canvas 28 × 25 in.
Petworth House

Three Marys in the Upton picture may derive from Michelangelo's *Crucifixion of St Peter* in the Cappella Paolina fresco, and the figure bent over the cross is based on one of the fishermen in Raphael's tapestry cartoon of *The Miraculous Draught of Fishes*.

How does *El Espolio* relate to the famous altar-piece in the sacristy of the Cathedral at Toledo of 1577–9? Does it precede this work, or was it painted afterwards as a by-product? El Greco's models were seen by Pacheco when he visited the painter in 1611, who described them as 'originals of all that he had painted in his life'. The expressive force of the picture and its sense of having been painted *alla prima* make it tempting to believe that it is a *modelle*. Differences occur between this smaller painting and the larger work; in the latter less sky appears and the man bent over the cross is more closely related to the rest of the composition. The Upton picture has a role in the history of taste. It almost certainly belonged to Delacroix, whose colours may owe much to the vivid tones of the Spanish Master. It was then in the possession of Baron Schwiter, Delacroix's executor, whose portrait by this artist is in the National Gallery.

Seventeenth-century Spanish painting is sparsely represented in the Trust's collection. However, the visitor to Dyrham, a house rich in souvenirs of the Anglo-Dutch connection of the second half of the seventeenth century, will be fascinated by the opportunity offered there of comparing Murillo's *Peasant Woman and Boy* and the copy after it which may be confidently attributed to Gainsborough. Murillo was immensely popular in the eighteenth century, in both France and England, and one of the first books on the artist was written by an Englishman, Captain Edward Davies, in 1819. However, Murillo's reputation led to the production of indifferent copies, and it is only when his originals are studied in some quantity, as in the Prado or the Seville Museum, that his silken elegance may be properly appreciated.

The Dyrham painting contains the elements that commend Murillo— a spacious, airy background, details of still life suggestive of the excellence of Spanish *bodegónes*, an alert dog that offers a comparison to those painted by Velázquez, and a charming lad. No wonder, then, that it attracted an eighteenth-century English artist. Tradition has it that the copy was done for William Blathwayt in 1760 by Gainsborough, a year after the painter had settled in Bath. The house is only a short distance from Bath, and Gainsborough was certainly keen on the Spanish Master, as is attested to by his 'fancy' pictures. The copy is lighter in tone than its prototype, and the warm colours are comparable to those in Gainsborough's early landscapes.

The debt of English artists to continental schools hardly needs labouring and this is especially evident in sixteenth- and seventeenth-century portrait-painting. Although Jacobean and Elizabethan portraiture had admirers in the 1890s and 1900s—Lionel Cust and Whistler for instance—it is only relatively recently that closer attention has been paid to it and the miniatures of Nicholas Hilliard and Isaac Oliver first properly studied by Basil Long.

A relationship with Oliver, for instance, may be observed in the full-length portrait of Richard Sackville, third Earl of Dorset, which, together with that of his wife, Lady Anne Clifford (pl. 8), hangs at Knole, a house intimately connected with English history. In former times, the portrait of the Earl was ascribed to either Daniel Mytens or Marcus Gheerhaerts. This and its companion have now been given to the artist whose personality has been reconstructed as William Larkin. He emerges as one of the major painters working in England during the period and responsible for the famous Redlynch set, now at Ranger's House, Blackheath. This contains another version of the portrait of Lord Dorset, as well as a portrait of his brother, the fourth Earl.

The third Earl, a close friend of James I, was notorious for his extravagance. His wife—one of the many remarkable women whose portraits are in the Trust's hands—later married the fourth Earl of Pembroke, but when this marriage proved unsuccessful she retired to hold sway over her own vast estates in Cumberland. She had a literary bent and kept a diary for the years 1616–19 which provides a detailed account of life at Knole and contains a mention of her having sat to Larkin for a portrait which she gave to her cousin and is presumably not the one at Knole. The charm of such portraits is due as much as anything else to the splendour of the costumes, both male and female, which have a touch of the fantasy of contemporary poetry, but they also resemble playing cards—court ones, of course. What a difference occurred when Van Dyck came to England.

Van Dyck has been somewhat dwarfed by the more robust and versatile figure of his fellow countryman and one-time master, Rubens. Yet his portraits often contain a poignancy and poetry rarely, if ever, found in those of Rubens. Van Dyck's Genoese portraits are remarkable, providing the image of a society in which the seeds of dissolution have already been sown; he could spot the canker in the rose. With alert sensitivity the Prince of Court Painters could penetrate the features of his sitters, particularly if he was in tune with their personalities.

The collection at Petworth contains two of Van Dyck's most effective portraits—the amazingly lively study of the Wizard Earl, Henry Percy, ninth Earl of Northumberland, and the no less revealing portrait of Thomas Wentworth, first Earl of Strafford (pl. 9). Once again the Trust's pictures show the debt of a then-modern master to the past, for the pose in this work is derived from Titian's *General del Vasto Addressing his Troops*—then in the possession of Charles I—and the allusion would have delighted the Whitehall set. The highlights on the armour are in the manner of Tintoretto.

This portrait, which almost certainly dates from 1636, was probably designed for Lady Carlisle, to whom Strafford was deeply attached, although their relationship may well have been platonic. Strafford was anxious for the painting to be a success; writing to his agent he said, 'mind Sir Anthony that he will take good pains upon the perfecting of the picture *with his own pencil.*' It is a brilliant psychological study, admirably bringing out the Earl's determination. Does it possess an intimation of his fate? This illustrious servant and staunch supporter of Charles I—he was Lord Deputy in Ireland—perished on the scaffold.

Van Dyck was responsive to beautiful women, so numerous at the Stuart Court. One of his most appealing female portraits, however, is not of an English beauty, but of the seductive Elizabeth or Teresia, a Circassian noble-woman married to 'Sir' Robert Shirley, whom Van Dyck also painted, a typical English adventurer who served as roving envoy for the Shah of Persia. Van Dyck met the couple in 1622 in Rome, where Shirley was engaged on a diplomatic mission. Both sitters wear oriental costume and the treatment of their gorgeous apparel shows the painter's allegiance to Venice rather than to Rome.

Like Van Dyck, Peter Lely was a gifted painter of women and one whose skill at capturing character, as well as charm, is revealed in the enchanting portrait at Ham House of Elizabeth Murray, Countess of Dysart (pl. 10). This 'stunner' is rumoured to have been the mistress of Oliver Cromwell, who, like many another revolutionary, did not disdain highborn ladies! This passionate and vivacious creature was known for her covetousness; she was 'a violent friend, and a much more violent enemy'. Her first husband was Sir Lionel Tollemache and her second, whom she married in 1672, the Duke of Lauder-dale. She had succeeded to Ham House (owned by the National Trust, but administered by the Victoria and Albert Museum) in about 1650 and after 1660 she obtained the title of Countess of Dysart in her own right. She may have had her faults, but she was a woman of taste, and this very Scottish *femme fatale* turned Ham into one of the most splendid interiors of the period.

Few paintings in the Trust's collection are as beautiful as Rubens's *The Garden of Love* (pl. 13) at Waddesdon, a work worthy of the Prado. The Waddes-don panel is possibly identical with *Een conversatie à la mode op panel* listed in Rubens's posthumous inventory of 1645, which was taken over by his widow Hélène Fourment at a valuation of 120 florins. The first certain record of the Waddesdon painting is to be found in the inventory, probably of the late eighteenth century, of the collection of the Duque de Infantando of Madrid, and in 1885 it was acquired by Baron Edmond de Rothschild from the Pastrana Palace in that city.

The late Ludwig Burchard maintained that the first version of the picture (which may be assessed by means of X-rays under the present surface) was probably painted in 1630–1. At this stage it contained neither steps nor balus-trade. Rubens arranged for the design to be published as a woodcut, but with modifications: the fountain and the two figures on the right were cut out, and a balcony with a pair of lovers disturbed by the play of water was substituted for the rosebush behind the central figures. The next stage, apparently, was the execution of the very large canvas in the Prado which includes, to quote Professor Ellis Waterhouse, 'a seated figure in the fountain, different Cupids in the air, a balcony with startled lovers in the background, and the omission of the second lady from the group at the right'. After these changes had taken place, Rubens painted the Waddesdon composition with the attention we now see.

The painting was not a public commission, but executed for the artist's own pleasure. The scene is set in the garden of an idealized version of his country house, the Château de Steen. Members of his family, cupids and a pair of lovers —doubtless symbolizing the master and his sixteen-year-old wife—are shown in a dream-like setting in which the real and the evocative generously inter-mingle.

Like much of Rubens's art, it attests to his profound culture, and the theme —a garden of love—goes back to fourteenth-century ivories and probably to fifteenth-century tapestries, and it looks ahead to the magical paintings of Watteau. Yet, though monumental in size, Rubens's picture is not static; it is endowed with a baroque swirl beloved of a master who had lived in Italy and kept abreast of modern currents; the movement suggests the heady impulse of passion.

English collectors were among the first outside Holland to appreciate its artistic Golden Age, and the national collections are rich in first-class examples of this school. Cuyp has long been a favourite in England and one of his most atmospheric paintings, the large *View of Dordrecht on the Maas* (pl. 12), is in the Trust's possession at Ascott. It was bought by Anthony de Rothschild at the famous Holford sale of 1928. First recorded in Sir George Colebrook's sale in 1774 as two pictures, it appeared again in Lady Stuart's sale at Christie's in 1841, the two pictures entitled *Morning* and *Evening*. They were acquired by a London dealer, Thomas Brown, who reunited them and sold the picture to James Holford. The painting, which probably dates from the 1650s, is justly famous, for Cuyp has captured the magic of evening light as it plays on a pic-turesque Dutch town with water and shipping. In this idyllic scene an intricate composition is rendered with deceptive simplicity by the use of silhouettes and the sort of envelope of soft light that would have appealed to Corot.

Dutch painters were in love with their surroundings, and many found a con-tinuous source of pride and inspiration in the depiction of their native land. What often fascinated them was the contrast between land, water and sky. Capelle, Van Goyen and Ruysdael, to name but three masters of the Dutch School, found endless subjects of this sort. The last-mentioned, for instance, is well represented in the collection at Ascott by *Le Coup de Vent* and at Polesden

7 Giovanni di Paolo (active 1420–82)   *Presentation of the Virgin*   panel 8 × 10 in.
Upton House

9 Sir Anthony van Dyck (1599–1641) *1st Earl of Strafford* canvas 52¾ × 43 in. Petworth House

8 William Larkin (active 1610–20) *Countess of Dorset* canvas 81 × 51¼ in. Knole

10 Sir Peter Lely (1618–80) *Elizabeth Murray, Countess of Dysart* canvas 48 × 39½ in. Ham House

11 Rembrandt (1606–69) *Portrait of a Man* canvas 37 × 29½ in. Buscot Park

12 Aelbert Cuyp (1620–91)   *Dordrecht on the Maas* (left side)   canvas 27 × 76 in.   Ascott

13 Sir Peter Paul Rubens (1577–1640)   *The Garden of Love*   panel 50 × 89 in.   Waddesdon Manor

14 El Greco (1541–1614)   *El Espolio*   panel 21 × 13 in.   Upton House

15 Pieter de Hoogh (1629–after 1684)   *The Game of Skittles*   canvas $27\frac{1}{2} \times 24\frac{1}{2}$ in.
Waddesdon Manor

16 Meindert Hobbema (1638–1709)
Cottages in a Wood   panel 23 × 33½ in.   Ascott

17 Nicolas de Largillière (1656–1746)
Sir Robert Throckmorton   canvas 53¾ × 41¼ in.
Coughton Court

18 Pompeo Batoni (1708–87)
Sir Matthew Fetherstonhaugh
canvas 39 × 29 in.   Uppark

19 William Hogarth (1647–1764)
The Holland House Group
canvas 50 × 40 in.   Ickworth

20 Claude (1600–1682)   *Landing of Aeneas at Pallanteum*   canvas 69 × 87¼ in.   Anglesey Abbey

21 George Stubbs, A.R.A. (1724–1806)   *Five Mares*   canvas 39 × 74 in.   Ascott

22 Thomas Gainsborough, R.A. (1727–88) *Duchess of Richmond* canvas 91 × 60 in.
Ascott

23 Sir Joshua Reynolds, P.R.A.
(1732–92)
David Garrick
canvas 30 × 25 in.
Knole

24 François Boucher (1703–70)
Philippe Égalité as a Child
canvas $35\frac{3}{4} \times 28\frac{1}{2}$ in.
Waddesdon Manor

25 Thomas Gainsborough, R.A. (1727–88)   *Augustus Hervey, 3rd Earl of Bristol*
canvas $91\frac{1}{2} \times 60$ in.   Ickworth

26 J. M. W. Turner, R.A. (1775–1851)   *Cockermouth Castle*   canvas $23\frac{3}{4} \times 35\frac{1}{2}$ in.
Petworth House

27 Samuel Scott (*c.* 1702–72)   *The Tower of London*   canvas 39×74 in.   Felbrigg Hall

28 Sir Edward Burne-Jones, A.R.A. (1833–98)   *Love Among the Ruins*   canvas $37\frac{1}{2} \times 63$ in.
Wightwick Manor

29 R. P. Bonington (1802–28) *Normandy Coast Scene* canvas 31 × 46¾ in. Anglesey Abbey

30 W. F. Witherington, R.A. (1785–1865) *Fête at Petworth* canvas 33 × 47½ in. Petworth House

31 William Blake (1757–1827) *The Cycle of the Life of Man* Watercolour 16 × 19½ in.
Arlington Court

Lacey by *The Zuider Zee Coast near Muiden*, in which the grey tonalities and wide expanse of the scene suggest the humid atmosphere of a sea now no more than a memory. The companion to this painting is in the National Gallery; both belonged to that keen eighteenth-century connoisseur of Dutch art, the Duc de Choiseul, and later to the Marquis de Marigny, Madame de Pompadour's brother, and 'Minister of Arts'.

The Dutch masters suggested the growth and power of Nature, and, in the same way as many oriental painters, they held trees in affection. None more so than Hobbema, who loved painting winding paths amid thick clumps of trees, as in *Cottages in a Wood* (pl. 16), at Ascott, which dates from about 1660 and was once in the famous Baring collection. This is one of those Dutch pictures that emphasizes the influence exerted by the Dutch School on French nine-teenth-century painting, that of Théodore Rousseau in particular. The couple seen in the path look ahead to the sort of subject which was painted by J. F. Millet, though the latter artist worked on a more monumental scale.

The Dutch painters revealed their love of nature in pictures of formal gardens and flowers. Pieter de Hoogh's *Game of Skittles* (pl. 15), of about 1665, at Waddesdon is a masterpiece of this genre, as subtle in colour as in content. In this exquisite evocation of patrician life, a pair of lovers—they are surely that— are shown gazing at each other in the carefully tended garden of a country house, their encounter being watched by a quizzical spectator. The scene may possess some erotic symbolic meaning and, in any event, it presents an idealized vision of life. Its charm lies in the careful positioning of the figures, and the enigmatic note is emphasized by the woman standing with her back to the spectator. How beautifully, too, the golden-toned costume of the woman is painted.

The role of love as portrayed in Dutch cabinet-painting ought to attract a special study. Ter Borch's *Duet*, 1675, also at Waddesdon, possesses a myster-ious touch evidenced by the strange figure in a shovel-hat who looks at the man playing music and courting his smartly dressed companion. Yet, although the subject is anecdotal, the picture is a work of art. Ter Borch's eye for tonal relationships allowed him to place his figures in atmospheric space, one reason why this painter appealed to Whistler. The humour which is also evident recalls how, in the eighteenth century, the Dutch School produced one of the wittiest artists of the period, Cornelis Troost.

During the disturbed times of the early nineteenth century, English dealers took the opportunity to acquire on the Continent many works of great import-ance. One especially active dealer was Samuel Woodburn, who later pur-chased Sir Thomas Lawrence's collection of Old Master drawings. It was he also who bought 'in an obscure village in Holland for a trifling sum' in 1817 one of the most memorable pictures belonging to the Trust—Rembrandt's deeply re-flective portrait of a man (pl. 11), now at Buscot, which was bought by the first

◀ 32 J. M. Rysbrack *Hercules*, 1744 Terracotta ht. 23½ in. Stourhead

Lord Faringdon in 1894. The old theory that it represents Jan Six is no longer tenable and it is now often considered to be of Clement de Jongh, a publisher of prints active in Amsterdam from 1650 until his death in 1679. He was the first known collector of Rembrandt's etchings, owning seventy-four; the artist did an etched portrait of him in 1651.

The features in both painting and print correspond, but the personality shown in each differs considerably. The man in the etching is an outgoing dominating character; the man in the oil is a prey to melancholy. How can this be explained? Either the portraits are of different people, or Rembrandt, with artistic licence, has endowed the sitter with what he felt was the true character that was masked by self-assertion. The portrait, which dates from the 1650s, when Rembrandt executed some of his finest works, is a splendid example of the chiaroscuro of which he was a master; a baroque ripple gives life to the hair.

Landscape flourished not only in Holland and Flanders during the seventeenth century, but also in Italy, with Annibale Carracci and Domenichino. The main exponents were foreigners, especially the French: Poussin, his brother-in-law Gaspard Dughet, and Claude. Dughet has long won admirers in England and his influence may be observed on John Wootton and Richard Wilson and on landscape gardens, notably that at Stourhead.

The collection at Stourhead contains two works by Dughet which once belonged to Henry Hoare, for whom they were bought by Horace Mann, the British Resident in Florence, in 1758. Mann secured them from the Arnaldi family for about £300 and, writing to Horace Walpole, he described them as having figures by Dughet's brother-in-law Niccolò, and as being larger 'than any I believe, except some at Versailles'. Hoare had asked him to secure Claudes 'at almost any price, but of the latter none are to be found'. Mann rightly pointed out that the two Dughets were rather dark and in none too good a condition. However, a melodious example of Dughet's painting is to be seen at Ickworth; it belonged to John, Lord Hervey by 1741.

Nevertheless, eighteenth-century English collectors were able to secure splendid examples of Claude's work, one of the most avid lovers of his Arcadian scenes being Thomas Coke, first Earl of Leicester; those he acquired are now in the present Lord Leicester's possession at Holkham. Political upheaval also brought to England two famous pictures by the Master now at Anglesey Abbey, *Landscape with the Father of Psyche Sacrificing to Apollo* and *The Landing of Aeneas at Pallanteum* (pl. 20). In 1798–9 when the French occupied Rome, the blind Prince Altieri disposed of these to two English dealers, Charles Grignion and Robert Fagan, who got them out of the city to Sicily. Nelson detached a frigate from the Mediterranean fleet to bring them to England, where they were acquired by William Beckford.

Among the many artists and connoisseurs who saw them in Beckford's town house where they were on show, entrance being by private ticket, was Turner. Joseph Farington, however, noted that when Turner viewed *The Father of Psyche* he was 'both pleased and unhappy ... it seemed beyond the power of imitation'. Claude's picture probably inspired his *Festival upon the Opening of the Vintage at Maçon*, 1803 (Graves Art Gallery, Sheffield). The appeal of the Altieri Claudes, which date from 1662 and 1675 respectively, is understandable. They are noble landscapes with a classical mood and are elegant in handling; they have an almost operatic touch, as if the curtain had just risen and the cast were about to burst into song.

Although French art of the eighteenth century was not so warmly patronized by English collectors—political differences disturbed the two countries—French influence was stronger on English art than was once believed: even such a 'true blue' as Hogarth derived inspiration from prints after de Troy.

One of the most colourful portraits by that sometimes underestimated French painter, Nicolas de Largillière, is of an Englishman, Sir Robert Throckmorton of Coughton Court (pl. 17), the fourth Baronet and a member of an old Warwickshire Catholic family which had been involved in intrigues against Queen Elizabeth and, indirectly, in the Gunpowder Plot. This vivacious and elegant work was painted in 1729, almost certainly in Paris, at the same time as the portraits of Throckmorton's sister Anne and two of her nieces, who took vows in the Paris house of the Augustinian 'Blue Sisters'. The portrait of Sir Robert was seen by Horace Walpole when it hung at Weston in Northamptonshire.

Probably there were more French eighteenth-century paintings in English hands than has been realized; we know for example that Watteau visited England in 1721 when he came to consult Dr Richard Mead, a notable physician and collector. However, most of the Trust's paintings from the *dixhuitième* were acquired in the nineteenth century and are at Waddesdon, including two associated with Watteau and five by his best pupil, Lancret—elegant examples of this painter's happy blending of the pastoral and rustic tradition, and of his love of the Italian Comedy.

Perhaps the most surprising French picture from this period belonging to the Trust is Boucher's portrait at Waddesdon of Philippe Egalité (then Duc de Montpensier) as a child (pl. 24). Only a seer could predict, however, that this little boy was to introduce jockeys, to play the part of a regicide, and to perish under the guillotine. It is a lively example of Boucher's technical dexterity, and his treatment of the toys looks back to his seventeenth-century predecessors in still life and ahead to Balthus.

The role of the English patron and collector in eighteenth-century Italy is a congenial theme which, deservedly, has attracted considerable attention. It was a golden moment for the milord with guineas in his pocket, and in Rome and elsewhere he found middlemen to guide his taste and help him to make purchases.

Lord Exeter, Sir Robert Walpole, and Lord Leicester were among those who acquired notable Roman and Bolognese baroque pictures. Yet how typical of the fortuitous nature of the Trust's collection that it contains few paintings from this school! Nevertheless, there is a Guercino of *Absalom and Tamar* at Tatton, which, however, does not show this master at his most polished.

An intriguing example of the late Roman baroque is Carlo Maratta's curious picture at Stourhead of the Marchese Pallavicini being introduced to the artist. This was painted in 1705 and was another work bought by Horace Mann for Henry Hoare. Mann told Walpole that he had secured it for 900 crowns 'though the old folks [the Arnaldi] always insisted on 2,000. I only wait for their getting a licence to send it away, for Richecourt made a law some years ago to prohibit the exportation of any valuable things of this nature, just as if the country was rich enough to prefer them to money.'

One house owned by the Trust, Uppark, contains a collection evocative of Rome and the Grand Tour. This delightful place was bought from its previous owners by Sir Matthew Fetherstonhaugh, who in 1746 succeeded to the immense fortune of a kinsman. When Fetherstonhaugh was in Rome, Reynolds included him in his celebrated parody of Raphael's *School of Rome*, which is now in the National Gallery of Ireland, and he sat to Pompeo Batoni (pl. 18), the Sargent of his age. He was not the only member of his family to have done so, and out of the twelve pictures by this master at Uppark, ten are portraits. He and his brother-in-law, Benjamin Lethieullier, were also patrons of Joseph Vernet, and six characteristic and delightful paintings by this artist are in the house.

English painting inevitably receives a good showing in the Trust's properties. The exhibition of Hogarth at the Tate Gallery in 1971–2 presented this versatile artist in the round—portraitist, conversation-painter, and master of the comic vein. One of his most entertaining paintings is the Holland House group (pl. 19) at Ickworth; it was painted in about 1737. It depicts leading members of the Whig party in the grounds of an unidentified country house. Lord Hervey, the Vice-Chamberlain of the King's Household, and a Tory, is shown rejecting a plan offered by Lord Holland, for whom he obtained the position of Surveyor of the King's Works in 1737. The man seated at the table is Lord Ilchester, who is shown tipping a clergyman into the water. This cleric is Peter Willemin, who is examining through a telescope a nearby church of which he had been offered the living, though failing to obtain it. The others represented are the Duke of Marlborough and Thomas Winnington.

Hogarth's talent for capturing the spirit of his age is admirably conveyed in the enchanting pictures *Morning* and *Night* at Upton, two of the series, 'The Four Times of the Day', painted in the 1730s. They provide a 'romantic' and humorous vision of eighteenth-century London with such scenes as Tom King's Coffee House and Covent Garden in the first, and the Rummer's Tavern ('The

New Bagnio') in the second. These works look ahead to the sort of comico-satirical work produced by Cruikshank.

In the seventeenth century, numerous Dutch painters left delightful records of Dutch towns and the genre expanded during the succeeding one. It was almost as if some artists had an unconscious intimation that before too long much of the most delectable architecture of their age, not to mention the elegance of the *ancien régime*, were to vanish: others, such as Hubert Robert and Pannini, relished the magic of ruins.

Fortunately Venice has altered less than most other cities, as the views painted by Canaletto and Guardi reveal. Both artists are represented in the Trust's collection. Canaletto's *Bacino di San Marco* (*c.* 1721–6) at Upton is an impressive and appealing vista of a famous scene and it is the sort of picture that influenced Guardi. By a fortunate coincidence evidence of the older artist's impact on the younger is confirmed by two early works of Guardi, at Waddesdon. They are his largest known pictures and also represent the Bacino di San Marco, although painted from different angles.

Canaletto's reputation among the English was considerable, largely thanks to the propaganda of Consul Joseph Smith, and like other Venetians— Pellegrini and the Riccis—this view-painter came to England. His *Chelsea from the Thames*, 1751, at Blickling is a tender view of a district rich in artistic associations which was to provide favourite themes for Whistler. Canaletto, like the American painter, was to create nocturnes—such as the two astonishing pictures now in the Berlin-Dahlem Gallery.

The relationship between Canaletto and Samuel Scott is obvious. They painted the same kind of scene and on one occasion the Venetian is known to have worked from drawings by the Englishman. Scott's two London scenes (pl. 27), of 1753, at Felbrigg are among the most accomplished in his *œuvre* and may be compared with the Paris views done by Raguenet or the Spanish scenes of Luis Paret y Alcazar, who is represented at Upton.

The student of English portraiture neglects the Trust's pictures at his peril. A painter such as J. M. Wright, who worked in Italy and the Netherlands, may be seen to advantage at Sudbury. The Trust's group of English portraits is impressive: magnates, beautiful women, great actors, famous authors, and commanders in the field and at sea. How to select favourites from such a galaxy? Should it be Romney's elegant full-length of William Beckford at Upton, or Reynolds's portrait at Knole of David Garrick (pl. 23), whose features were notoriously difficult to capture, or the same artist's Oliver Goldsmith? The Trust's collection, in any event, permits contrasts to be made; for instance, between Reynolds's *Third Duke of Dorset* at Knole and Gainsborough's *Third Earl of Bristol* (pl. 25) at Ickworth, which Walpole characterized as 'very good' and one of the 'best modern pictures', or between Reynolds's *Theresa Robinson, Mrs Parker* at Saltram, an example of the President of the

Royal Academy's neo-classical taste, and Gainsborough's *Duchess of Richmond* (pl. 22) at Ascott.

Equestrian and sporting pictures find their place in the Trust's varied collection. How appropriate that the Trust owns (at Ascott) Stubbs's *Five Mares* (pl. 21), *c.* 1765, in which the national love of the horse is given in essence. The composition, an elegant frieze, is informed by the naturalness that marks many portraits of the time.

The evolution of English landscape-painting is a fascinating subject. It owed much to foreign example in the early stages, and as late as the eighteenth century men such as Wilson and Gainsborough were considerably influenced by Italian and Dutch painting. Yet both artists evolved their individual styles; Wilson is represented in the Trust's collection by two typically English scenes, *A View of the Deer* at Petworth and *A View of Windsor Forest*, of the 1770s, at Anglesey, which is painted with warm colour and cool shadows.

English collectors could be perceptive in their patronage. For instance, Sir Richard Colt Hoare, the historian of Wiltshire and author of tours of Italy and Sicily, almost certainly commissioned J. R. Cozens, most poetic of water-colourists, to paint the two views of the Pays de Valais, near Geneva, and Lake Nemi, now at Stourhead. However, Hoare was a minor patron compared with the third Earl of Egremont, who was one of the first to spot the genius of Turner. This artist had a studio at Petworth and painted dreamy views of the grounds. Egremont owned other works by him, such as the brilliant *Cockermouth Castle* (pl. 26), of 1810, one of the many masterpieces by Turner in this collection.

Although the Trust owns only one painting by Constable (at Anglesey Abbey), by no means his best effort, it also possesses in the same collection a luminous canvas by Bonington, *Normandy Coast Scene* (pl. 29) painted in 1826. This once belonged to Baron Rivet, with whom Bonington visited Italy in that year. It has the brilliance of colour that meant much to Delacroix.

The Trust's collection also contains first-class works by unfamiliar painters. Thus, at Petworth may be found an enchanting picture of the fête held in the park in 1835 (pl. 30), when Lord Egremont was eighty-four: he is on horseback to the left—a true Duke of Omnium. How well the artist, W. F. Witherington, has evoked the delightful atmosphere of the occasion, and, when a similar event was held in the previous year, Charles Greville, the famous diarist, described it as being 'altogether one of the gayest and most beautiful spectacles I ever saw'.

Poetic painting is a characteristically English tradition. The Trust owns four works by its chief exponent—William Blake—three of which are at Petworth, *Satan calling up the legions*, which was executed for Lady Egremont; *The Last Judgement*, which shows the artist's debt to Michelangelo; and *Characters from Spenser's Faerie Queen*. The fourth, the so-called *Cycle of the Life of Man* (pl. 31), of 1821, was only discovered in 1949 at Arlington Court and is pertinent to an understanding of Blake's beliefs, since it has been held to epitomize his neo-platonic philosophy, showing the regeneration or the 'descent and return of souls'.

The main emphasis in the Trust's collections falls on the Old Masters. However, collectors such as the first Lord Faringdon and Sir Geoffrey Mander acquired works by the Pre-Raphaelites, which are shown at Buscot and Wightwick Manor. Burne-Jones is especially well represented by his famous *Briar Rose* series (Buscot) and by *Love Among the Ruins* (pl. 28), which is an oil version done in 1894 of a water-colour of 1873. It was acquired by Lord Bearsted and is now exhibited at Wightwick Manor. Such pictures possess the languorous elegance of this master of the *fin de siècle*, who was one of the few English painters of his time to win a reputation on the Continent.

3

Sculpture

John Kenworthy-Browne

Sculpture in National Trust houses falls conveniently into the period 1700–1850. Almost, that is, but not quite; for, although the English tradition grew and flowered during the 150 years between Francis Bird and Sir Francis Chantrey, it took root earlier and withered later. Portrait busts were also made during the seventeenth century; and a hundred years ago the habit of putting monumental bronze and marble in country seats was not quite dead. The tradition was sufficiently broken, however, to allow many owners cheerfully, and often disastrously, to neglect their sculptural inheritance. If space were to be cleared or money raised, sculpture was generally the first thing to go: either to decay in gardens and storehouses, or to lose its identity in salerooms and sometimes to disappear altogether.

Not every house contains sculpture as it does furniture and paintings, for the formation of a sculpture collection was the mark of a patron both wealthy and discriminating, who could not only acquire marbles but provide a worthy setting for them. Sculpture makes peculiar demands on a house: it requires space and air. Portrait busts, when crowded together, can be ineffective; figures and groups must be seen from different angles, must be suitably placed as to height, and carefully lit. Sculpture generally has a monumental quality unsuited to the boudoir or drawing-room. It was usually placed in the hall, staircase or library, or perhaps in a specially designed gallery, as at Petworth.

The art of the portrait bust, first fully developed in ancient Rome, was revived at the Renaissance. However, examples dating from before the middle of the seventeenth century are rare in English country houses. Hence the interest of a bronze portrait of the Countess of Dysart (pl. 35), made as early as about 1630, at Ham House. It has all the forceful character of a court lady approaching middle age. If, as is thought, it was made in England, it was probably by the Frenchman, Hubert Le Sueur (who worked *c.* 1610–51). He came to England at the invitation of Charles I, and brought with him the practice of bronze portraiture. At Stourhead, the Trust owns a gilt-bronze bust of Charles I (pl. 34), also by Le Sueur. It seems to have been at Stourhead since the early eighteenth century, but in 1638 it was at Whitehall Palace and belonged to the King himself. Cromwell sold it with the other royal treasures, and it was probably during the Commonwealth period that the bronze was covered with dark varnish. This has recently been removed, and the bust shows once again its original gilding.

During the eighteenth century, the best marble busts were almost invariably made in London, and for this reason alone a marble portrait implies that the sitter was cosmopolitan and urbane. At Hanbury Hall there is a bust of the owner and builder, the lawyer Thomas Vernon, who died in 1721. He is shown in typical baroque style, with a plump face and a curling, full-bottomed wig. Although neither signed nor dated, it is thought to be a posthumous portrait, made by Francis Bird (1667–1731). There are no other marbles in the house, but the Vernons continued to patronize sculptors, and the fine family monuments in the parish church, including works by Roubiliac and Chantrey, should not be missed by the visitor. At Sudbury Hall there is an unsigned portrait bust of Admiral Vernon, a distant relative of the Vernons of Hanbury, which is attributed to Rysbrack. A pair of busts at Shugborough of Admiral Lord Anson and his Lady, also unsigned, have been attributed, though not convincingly, to either Roubiliac or Wilton. And at West Wycombe Park there is yet another unsigned bust, c. 1750, of Sir Francis Dashwood (Lord Le Despencer), who is shown with an open shirt, and a cap in place of his wig (pl. 38). This informal treatment was typical of the rococo group of artists who worked around St Martin's Lane. It is thought to have been carved by Sir Robert Taylor (1714–88), who abandoned sculpture in about 1753 to become an architect.

Two full-length statues are exceptional among the Trust's portrait sculpture. At The Vyne, among a haphazard collection of eighteenth- and nineteenth-century marbles, there is a magnificent commemorative work, the recumbent figure of Challoner Chute (d. 1659), which is placed in the Tomb Chamber next to the Chapel (pl. 39). Designed by Thomas Carter (d. 1795) in a vigorous style that contains no hint of classicism, the monument was ordered by John Chute, Challoner's great-grandson, about 1775. The fine carving may have been done by John Bacon (1740–99). At Knole, a very different kind of portrait comes as a surprise to the visitor. This is a female nude, lying on a mattress, cast in plaster and attributed to the Italian, J. B. Locatelli (c. 1735–1805); it is a portrait of the dancer, Gianetta Bacelli, who was for a time the mistress of the third Duke of Dorset. The Duke also had her painted, this time discreetly clothed, by Gainsborough in 1782.

If the Trust possesses no bust by Roubiliac, the finest rococo sculptor in London, there is ample compensation in the magnificent series of works by his slightly older rival, John Michael Rysbrack (1694–1770). This sculptor came to England from Antwerp in 1720, and was much patronized by the

E

Palladian-minded aristocracy and by Lord Burlington. A terracotta *Goat* (pl. 36) at Anglesey Abbey, which the sculptor himself described as 'one of the best things I have ever modelled', was the half-size maquette for a statue ordered by Lord Burlington for the garden at Chiswick House. The marble is now at Chatsworth. Rysbrack's splendid bust of Lord Bolingbroke at Petworth is in his best and noblest classical style; another version of this bust, dated 1737, survives at Bolingbroke's seat, Lydiard Tregoze, in Wiltshire.

Rysbrack's name will always be associated with Stourhead, where Henry Hoare, the creator of the Pleasure Grounds, became one of his most constant patrons. Hoare ordered no portrait of himself, but he bought mythological statues, a bust of King Alfred (who had rallied his army on the Stourhead estate), and, at the sculptor's posthumous sale, five classical reliefs and a number of drawings. Two portrait busts of Milton, now at Stourhead, were apparently ordered by Hoare's father-in-law, the Palladian architect William Benson. Benson's professional career was short and inglorious; he behaved shabbily to both Wren and St Paul's Cathedral. But in 1738 he commissioned Rysbrack to make the monument to Milton in Westminster Abbey, at the same time ordering the two Milton busts for himself. That of the blind and aged poet was based on the portrait by Faithorne; and the youthful bust, on the oil portrait that is now in the National Portrait Gallery. This had been painted when Milton, on account of his beauty, was known at Cambridge as 'the Lady of Christ's.'

Henry Hoare ordered two statues for the Temple of Hercules (known as the 'Pantheon') in his Pleasure Grounds. *Flora* (1760) is a reduced and more slender version of the massive antique statue now in Naples. The *Hercules*, ordered in 1747, was considered by Horace Walpole to be Rysbrack's *'chef d'oeuvre ...* an exquisite summary of his skill, knowledge and judgement.' The terracotta statuette or model of Hercules, made in 1744 and now also at Stourhead (pl. 32), is perhaps finer even than the finished marble. In his will the sculptor bequeathed it to Henry Hoare. Walpole described how, in order to make it, Rysbrack went to Broughton's gymnasium (off Tottenham Court Road) and modelled the different parts from various limbs of the strongest and best-formed men he could find. These were the bruisers and prizefighters of the day, and, Walpole continued, 'as the games of that Olympic academy frequently terminated to its heroes at the gallows, it was soon after suppressed by Act of Parliament; so that in reality Rysbrack's Hercules is the monument of those gladiators.'

From 1750, if not before, English sculptors were increasingly dominated by the examples remaining from classical times. By the end of the eighteenth century, in contrast to the lively features and courtly gestures of the baroque and rococo, the mark of fine sculpture was the nobility, simplicity and economy shown in the work of the ancients. Many talented sculptors went to Rome to study style and technique; collectors bought ancient works, either while on the Grand Tour, or afterwards through agents in Rome such as Gavin Hamilton and the none-too-honest Thomas Jenkins. Many houses, such as Powis Castle, West Wycombe and Stourhead, have a few such figures or fragments. But a gallery of classical marbles remains at Petworth House, such as only wealthy collectors like the second Earl of Egremont could afford. Not many such private galleries survive in England, and, accustomed as we are to the great national collections, we tend now to underrate those at Holkham, Newby and Petworth, and to regard with disfavour the eighteenth-century custom of entirely restoring missing legs, arms and noses. But the standard at Petworth is high, and among its treasures is a head of Aphrodite (pl. 33), attributed to Praxiteles, the Greek sculptor of the fourth century B.C.

Modern copies of ancient statues were also bought in Rome, or modern versions of classical subjects. At Powis there is a series of ten busts of the Caesars, carved in about 1750 by some anonymous Italian, who made up their tunics from coloured marble fragments removed from ancient buildings. Meanwhile, in London, John Cheere (1709–87) built up a considerable business in making ornamental figures in lead and plaster at his yard near Hyde Park Corner. Cheere's plaster heads of the Caesars may be seen at West Wycombe Park. At Uppark, six classical plaster heads were ordered from Cheere in 1759; while at Felbrigg, bronzed plaster heads of ancient and modern poets were supplied in 1752 to fit in with James Paine's stucco-work. Plaster sculpture was much used in interior decoration in the late eighteenth century. At Osterley, Adam designed the niches in the hall to contain plaster casts of classical statues. Between 1812 and 1815 Repton redesigned the dining-room at Uppark to include plaster busts which were made by George Garrard (1760–1826), who had already worked for Foxite patrons at Woburn Abbey and Southill.

The marble bust of Pope Clement XIV at Beningbrough was made in Rome by the expatriate Irish sculptor, Christopher Hewetson (c. 1739–98). It is dated 1771, and is still in the baroque style rather than in his later neo-classical manner. This Pope founded the Pio Clementino Museum in the Vatican, and was later to dissolve the Jesuit order; yet it seems strange that Englishmen should have wanted his portrait. During the neo-classical period, the English sculptors most in demand for portrait busts were Nollekens and Chantrey. Joseph Nollekens (1737–1823) spent ten years (1760–70) in Rome, where he lived frugally and began to make his legendary fortune by restoring, selling and copying antiquities. Whilst there, he helped several Englishmen, including Thomas Anson of Shugborough, to form their collections of classical statuary; but unfortunately nearly all the Shugborough marbles were sold in 1842. When Nollekens returned to England he still had forty-five working years ahead of him. The busts of the Duke of Bedford at Shugborough, Lord Boringdon at Saltram, and the third Earl of Egremont at

Petworth (pl. 42), all of which were greatly admired, were made after 1800. His 'stock pieces', very often to be repeated, were of Fox and Pitt, and examples exist at Felbrigg, whose owner, William Windham (his monument by Nollekens is in the nearby church), was Minister of War under Pitt. At Ickworth, too, there are political busts by, or after, Nollekens, of Fox, Pitt, Canning and the Earl of Liverpool.

It is time to look at the mythological or 'ideal' sculpture of the neo-classical period. From 1781 until his death in 1822, Antonio Canova became the most renowned artist to have worked since Michelangelo. He was much patronized by the English. One of his earliest patrons was Lord Cawdor, for whom in 1789 he completed his *Amorino* (pl. 41). This exquisite image of Love was lost early in the last century. It had been, apparently, standing in a garden for many years before Lord Fairhaven bought it, unrecognized, about twenty-five years ago for Anglesey Abbey, and it was identified as Canova's youthful work only recently. In spite of the badly weathered surface, one can understand the admiration it caused when it first arrived in London.* There are also versions of Canova's works at Attingham Park, namely the Italian Venus and a head of Hebe, bought by Lord Berwick in 1926.

The eccentric Earl-Bishop of Bristol was an indefatigable traveller and collector in Italy. During the 1770s, Hewetson carved his portrait bust, which is at Ickworth (pl. 37). During his last, long visit to Italy the Earl-Bishop ordered Ickworth to be built in his absence, intending the rotunda to be an art gallery; and, about 1790, he commissioned a large marble group from John Flaxman (1755–1826), who was then studying in Rome. The work reached England safely, but the bulk of the great collection intended for Ickworth was seized by the French revolutionary army and dispersed. Flaxman's *Fury of Athamas* is an ambitious work which put the sculptor to great trouble and expense; but he was never at his best showing figures in motion, and the work has not been popular. This great artist's masterpiece of ideal sculpture, *St Michael overcoming Satan* (pl. 48), completed for the third Earl of Egremont some thirty years later, is still the central exhibit in the gallery at Petworth.

After the overthrow of Napoleon in 1814, the English were able once more to travel to Italy, where they ordered quantities of fine sculpture from Canova, Thorvaldsen and others. But Lord Egremont was patriotic, and would not give commissions to foreign artists. Already a liberal collector of English paintings, the septuagenarian Earl had enlarged his gallery at Petworth by 1823, and begun to order works from English sculptors, which were to stand beside the classical marbles collected by his father, the second Earl. No other patron ordered English sculpture on such a scale. There are two works by Flaxman,

* Canova completed another *Amorino* in 1793 for an Irishman, Mr La Touche, which also is missing. We prefer to think that the figure at Anglesey was Lord Cawdor's version.

33 attrib. Praxiteles   *Aphrodite*, Greek, 4th century B.C.   Marble, ht (without base) 25½ in.
Petworth House

34 Hubert Le Sueur   *Charles I, c.* 1635   Bronze, ht 27 in.   Stourhead

35 Hubert Le Sueur   *Catherine Bruce, Countess of Dysart, c.* 1630   Bronze, ht 31½ in.   Ham House

36 J. M. Rysbrack   *Reclining Goat, c.* 1730   Terracotta, ht 15 in., l. 28 in.   Anglesey Abbey

37 Christopher Hewetson   *Bishop of Derry,*
4th Earl of Bristol, c. 1770   Marble, ht 26½ in.
Ickworth

38 Sir Robert Taylor   *Lord Le Despencer, c.* 1750
Marble, ht 32 in.   West Wycombe Park

39 Marble monument to Chaloner Chute (d. 1659) designed by Thomas Carter, *c.* 1770–80
The Vyne

40 J. C. F. Rossi   *Celadon and Amelia, c.* 1820   Marble, ht 72 in.   Petworth House

41 Antonio Canova   *Amorino, c.* 1789   Marble, ht 4 ft 8 in.   Anglesey Abbey ▶

42 Joseph Nollekens (1737–1823) *3rd Earl of*
Egremont Marble, ht 22 in.
Petworth House

43 J.-B. Lemoyne *Mme de Pompadour*, 1761
Marble, ht 28½ in. Waddesdon Manor

44 and 45 William Behnes *Mr and Mrs George Hammond Lucy*, 1830 Marble, ht 29 in. Charlecote Park

46 R. J. Wyatt *Flora with Zephyr*, 1834
Marble, ht 7 ft 9 in.   Nostell Priory

47 Clodion *Votaries of Bacchus, c.* 1780
Terracotta, ht 20 in.   Waddesdon Manor

48 John Flaxman
St Michael overcoming Satan,
1826   Marble, ht 10 ft 1 in.
Petworth House

including the *St Michael* group; two by Sir Richard Westmacott (1775–1856); and two by J. C. F. Rossi (1762–1839), who also carved a seated Venus from a plaster model by Nollekens. Rossi's works are the uncouth pugilist known as *The British Athlete,* and a group, *Celadon and Amelia* (pl. 40), which depicts a pastoral tragedy from Thomson's *Seasons*. The lovers are overtaken by a storm; Celadon promises Amelia his protection, only to find her struck dead by lightning the same instant. The other sculptor represented at Petworth is the Irishman, John Edward Carew (1785–1868), who attracted Lord Egremont by his natural talent and charm. He made several family busts and five mythological works; but in some of these he overreached himself, and two outrageous heaps of marble are now relegated to the tenants' hall. Carew's prices proved to be as monstrous as his sculpture, and he lost a lawsuit against Lord Egremont's executors.

Richard James Wyatt (1795–1850) was one of two sculptors (the other being John Gibson) who went to study under Canova in Rome, where they remained and died. At Nostell Priory, Wyatt's large marble group of *Flora with Zephyr* (pl. 46) is a feat of virtuosity. It has something of Canova's emotional style, tempered by the decorative sentiments of the nineteenth century, and was probably the same as the group which Wyatt exhibited at the Royal Academy in 1834. It is not known when or how this group reached Nostell; but there it stands, isolated yet not unhappy, among eighteenth-century tapestries and Chippendale furniture.

Some of the English visitors to Italy after 1814 had their portrait busts made abroad. Those of the first Marquess and Marchioness of Bristol, at Ickworth, were made in Florence by Lorenzo Bartolini (1777–1850), who had been a pupil of J. L. David in Paris. With his fiery, independent temper, Bartolini had supported the Napoleonic regime, and his conversion, after 1815, to a natural and lyrical style, opposed to Canova's classicism, is hard to understand. Meanwhile, in England, the ability of Sir Francis Chantrey (1781–1841) to turn marble into flesh and feature was unsurpassed. Chantrey's bust of the Duke of Wellington, with its odd, upward turn of the head, is at Petworth. Some of his contemporaries, however, considered William Behnes (1795–1864) to be superior. Behnes was much patronized by the Royal family, and his fine pair of busts at Charlecote of Mr and Mrs George Lucy (1830) bear witness to his talents (pls. 44, 45). The hint of feminine affectation in Mary Lucy doubtless suited the taste of the day. At Hughenden Manor there is a portrait by Behnes of Disraeli, dated 1849. Another fine sculptor was Samuel Joseph (1791–1850), whose posthumous bust of William Huskisson, 1831, the statesman and victim of the first railway accident, is at Petworth.

Nothing has yet been said of French eighteenth-century sculpture, for with the exception of Waddesdon Manor there is relatively little in the Trust's houses. It certainly is quite different in character from the pieces already mentioned. Even Bouchardon's bust of John Lord Hervey (1729) at Ickworth, though it is in the 'antique style', seems to belong to another world from the marbles which surround it. French eighteenth-century portraits, especially those of the rococo Louis XV period, have an appearance not so much of lapidary dignity as of well-bred affability. In the Rothschild collection at Waddesdon, Lemoyne's portrait bust (pl. 43) of Madame de Pompadour (1761) seems to have overheard some pleasing remark, perhaps about the marquetry furniture, the Savonnerie or the Sèvres. The fine marbles at Waddesdon include works by Caffieri, Falconet, Pajou, Pigalle and others, and they would look strangely odd were they in an English rather than a French setting. In addition there are no less than seven terracottas by Clodion. The virtuosity of these erotic boudoir pieces is astonishing and their sentiments differ from those of traditional English taste. Satyrs, nymphs and bacchantes (pl. 47) disport themselves in the never-never land of some golden age, innocent of the troubles, rivalries and vexations of civilization.

4

Tapestry and Needlework

Donald King

Tapestries and needlework contributed much of the colour, pattern, warmth and comfort which are indispensable to a civilized interior. Small wonder, then, that the houses of the National Trust contain countless treasures of this kind. But it is a heritage which presents problems. These frail old textiles need to be carefully protected from dirt and light, which fade and destroy them. They require cleaning and conservation, amounting sometimes to hundreds of hours of painstaking labour on a single piece. Yet preserved they must be, not only because they are rare and beautiful things, but also because they retain the touch of living, breathing humanity in houses which, without them, might seem cold and lifeless.

The Tudor period

Tapestry emerged as a major art and a supremely important element of interior decoration in the fourteenth and fifteenth centuries, when the workshops of Arras, Tournai, Brussels and other neighbouring centres began to weave and to export throughout western Europe sets of hangings which were designed by painters and depicted, on a monumental scale, scenes of scripture, history, romance and hunting. Of the thousands of such tapestries which hung in English houses by the early Tudor period most have long since been destroyed, and the rare survivors have generally been removed elsewhere, like the fifteenth-century *Hunts* set formerly at Hardwick Hall, now in the Victoria and Albert Museum, or the fine group of tapestries of about 1500 formerly at Knole and now in America. A remnant of the enormous royal collection still remains at Hampton Court, but none of the Trust's medieval or early Tudor houses can boast a single contemporary tapestry.

A few characteristic examples from that period can, however, be seen in houses of somewhat later date. Two late fifteenth-century pieces, bequeathed to the Trust by Sir Malcolm Stewart, are at Montacute House. One of these, no doubt a fragment from a large set, depicts three episodes from the story of Hercules, a favourite theme in tapestry of that time, and illustrates the vigorously expressive narrative style then practised at Tournai and other centres. The second piece is a handsome example of the admirably decorative *millefleurs* style (pl. 49). Across a dark background sprinkled with a myriad flowers advances a figure marvellously evocative of that age, an armoured knight on a richly caparisoned horse, bearing a *gonfalon* charged with a ferocious beast and the enigmatic device IE. In one corner are the arms of the French nobleman Jean de Daillon and the piece is probably one of a set of verdure tapestries known to have been woven for him as a gift from the town of Tournai in 1481–2. *Millefleurs* and other verdure tapestries of the early and middle sixteenth century are displayed on the main stairs at Hardwick, along with two early sixteenth-century figurative hangings, namely a fragmentary *Lion Hunt,* probably from a Tournai set, and a large tapestry with scenes from the story of *David and Solomon,* exemplifying the densely packed compositions of stately elongated figures which were favoured in Brussels at this time.

A curious tapestry dated 1545, at Powis Castle, depicting a nearly contemporary event, the reception of a Venetian embassy by a turbaned oriental potentate, is closely based on extant Venetian paintings of the same subject and may serve as a reminder of the influence of Italian paintings on Flemish tapestry design in the sixteenth century. It was above all Raphael's cartoons for the *Acts of the Apostles,* woven in Brussels 1515–19, which led designers to abandon the stiff, late medieval manner of the Hardwick *David and Solomon* and adopt a new style of powerful, muscular figures moving freely in a deep pictorial space, framed by ornamental borders. This style can be seen in the great *Abraham* set, possibly designed by Bernard van Orley, which has hung at Hampton Court since the time of Henry VIII.

The evolution of the new style in the later sixteenth century and its regression towards less three-dimensional, more linear effects are well illustrated at Hardwick, where no fewer than six Flemish sets give a unique impression of the use of tapestries in a great house of the Elizabethan age. Bess of Hardwick, Countess of Shrewsbury, who built this house between 1591 and 1597, clearly attached great importance to the tapestries, for several of the principal rooms seem designed to display particular sets. The High Great Chamber, for instance, was apparently designed to take the fine Brussels set of eight *Ulysses* tapestries (pl. 62), which she had bought in 1587, and the Gallery for the thirteen enormous *Gideon* tapestries, woven for Sir Christopher Hatton in 1578 and bought by Bess from his heir in 1592. The latter set, originally the principal ornament of the Gallery, can now hardly be seen for the portraits which later generations have hung upon it ('bad tapestry, and worse pictures' was Horace Walpole's caustic comment, from the standpoint of a different age). Other sets still in the rooms where they were recorded in the Hardwick inventory of 1601 are the so-called *Esther* set (likewise woven for Hatton) and the *Planets,* while those of *David* and *Abraham* have been moved to different rooms; the last-named set, bought by Bess in 1592, has designs adapted from those of the Hampton Court *Abraham* set, which has been mentioned above.

A very delicate and fanciful tapestry style, suggesting the atmosphere of the Elizabethan and Jacobean masque, was practised in the workshop of François Spierincx, established first in Antwerp and later in Delft; it can be seen in the *Diana* set (pl. 57), in the Venetian Ambassador's bedroom at Knole, which may be a remnant of a larger set of this subject ordered from Spierincx by Sir Walter Raleigh in 1593.

Other houses of the Trust possessing one or more tapestries of the sixteenth century include Castle Drogo, Cotehele, Coughton Court, Great Chalfield Manor, Nunnington Hall, Packwood House, Polesden Lacey and Tattershall Castle. The productions of the small tapestry workshop set up by the Sheldon family of Warwickshire are represented by two little cushion-covers, one of *Judith* at Packwood and the other of the *Adoration of the Kings* at Fenton House; another sixteenth-century Sheldon design, a large-scale map including an interesting view of Elizabethan London, is reproduced in a mid-seventeenth-century English tapestry on loan at Oxburgh Hall.

Cheaper substitutes for tapestry were the painted cloths often mentioned in Elizabethan literature; a unique set painted with scenes from the life of *St Paul* is in the chapel at Hardwick. Painting and gilding were also used for flags and banners; an example associated with Sir Francis Drake can be seen at Buckland Abbey.

English embroidery and needlework of the Tudor period are superbly represented in National Trust houses. A finely embroidered ecclesiastical cope traditionally associated with Catherine of Aragon is preserved at Coughton Court and other examples of embroidery from pre-Reformation vestments can be seen at Hardwick, while at Cotehele there are interesting embroidered altar-hangings with figures of Christ, Apostles and Saints, and the arms of Sir Piers Edgcumbe and his first wife Jane Durnford (d. 1520). A sixteenth-century pillow-cover at Petworth, beautifully embroidered with flowers and heraldry, is romantically attributed to Lady Jane Grey. At Oxburgh Hall there is a famous set of green velvet wall-hangings with applied needlework panels depicting animals, plants and emblematic devices, signed by Mary, Queen of Scots, and Bess of Hardwick; one is dated 1570 (pl. 50). Other panels of Mary's needlework are at Hardwick Hall and a lace-trimmed chemise of hers is at Coughton Court. Hardwick retains an astonishing amount of the furnishing embroidery recorded there in 1601, much of it originally made by Bess and her household for Chatsworth, when she was furnishing that house in the 1570s. It includes two sets of velvet wall-hangings (one of them dated 1573) embroidered with large-scale figures of *Heroines* and *Virtues* (pl. 51). There are several needlework table-covers, including one of 1574 with the *Judgment of Paris*, one of 1579 with the story of *Tobit*, and others with armorial and grotesque patterns. There are also pictorial valances, parts of bed-hangings and many other pieces. The numerous needlework cushion-covers (pl. 52), some of which were on window-seats in the gallery in 1601, include scriptural, mythological, armorial and floral designs, while other cushion-covers are made from rich Italian brocades.

The Stuart period

Although no single house gives so complete a picture of the use of textiles in a Stuart interior as Hardwick does for the Elizabethan period, nevertheless a great wealth of original material is available in houses such as Knole, Cotehele, Ham, Lyme, Powis, and Dyrham. The classical harmony of early Renaissance textile and tapestry designs was still respected, but a trend towards exuberant baroque effects made itself felt, only to be curbed towards the end of the period by a more decorous taste, which did not, however, exclude a vein of oriental fantasy.

In 1620 a tapestry factory was set up at Mortlake and for a brief period, thanks to the lavish patronage of the court, produced some of the finest tapestries in Europe. To this period belongs the set of *Hero and Leander* at Lyme Park, which bear the FC mark of the factory's first director, Sir Francis Crane (d. 1636); the set, from cartoons by the factory designer, Francis Cleyn of Rostock, was often rewoven in less fine versions later in the century and examples can be seen at Hardwick, Cotehele and Anglesey Abbey. Apart from new designs such as these, much of the Mortlake production was based on sixteenth-century cartoons, such as Raphael's *Acts of the Apostles,* which were acquired for the use of the factory in 1623 and are now displayed—still part of the royal collection—at the Victoria and Albert Museum. Another example of this use of Italian Renaissance designs is the *Supper at Emmaus* in the Chapel at Hardwick, based on a famous Titian from Charles I's collection now in the Louvre. In the economic troubles leading to the Civil War the Mortlake factory declined, but some activity continued under the Commonwealth, when one project was for an *Abraham* set based on the sixteenth-century Flemish set at Hampton Court, already mentioned; a Mortlake set answering this description is at Blickling. Another set of sixteenth-century Flemish designs, the *Twelve Months,* first woven at Mortlake 1623–4, was repeatedly rewoven later; there are good examples at Clandon, West Wycombe and Ham (pl. 55), the last-named datable from its heraldry as late as 1699–1719.

From the 1670s onwards old Mortlake designs such as these seem to have been shared among several workshops, one of which was at the Great Wardrobe at Hatton Garden. A set of *Playing Boys* (pl. 53) at Hardwick, from designs by Cleyn inspired by sixteenth-century Italian models, have an inscription F. P. HATTON GARDEN, the mark of Francis Poyntz (d. 1685). The mark T. P. for Thomas Poyntz, active at the same period, appears on a set of *Nebuchadnezzar,* in the contemporary Flemish style, in the King's Bedroom at Knole; another set of the same subject is at Powis. Some English tapestries with the arms of the Duke of Lauderdale (d. 1682), possibly intended as table-covers, are at Ham. A novel type of *chinoiserie,* with small exotic figures on monochrome backgrounds as in oriental lacquers (pl. 54), was produced from 1690 onwards by, among others, John Vanderbank, who was director of the Great Wardrobe in Great Queen Street, London, from 1689 to 1727; there are tapestries of this class at The Vyne and Beningbrough. Vanderbank and others also employed foreign designs of recent date, such as the *Elements* after Le Brun or the *Venus* set after Albani; an English tapestry from the former series can be seen at Shugborough and two from the latter at Anglesey Abbey. Another foreign-inspired set, frequently woven, were the landscape tapestries with *Philosophers* (pl. 59), examples of which are at Dyrham Park and Antony.

Despite the efforts of the English workshops, imports of foreign, particularly Flemish, tapestries continued unabated and examples of these in houses of the Trust are so numerous that only a few can be selected for brief mention here. In Flanders, as elsewhere, some seventeenth-century sets were reworkings of sixteenth-century designs; this is the case with the fine Brussels set of *Hunts* at Upton. But as the seventeenth century advanced, Flemish production was strongly influenced by the designs of Rubens and Jordaens, full of bulky figures in vigorous movement, bursting out of a picture-space framed by swelling baroque borders. A Flemish set of *Achilles,* after designs by Rubens, is at Nunnington, while designs by Jordaens can be seen in a Brussels set of *Country Life* at Hardwick. A fine Bruges tapestry of *Rebecca at the Well* (pl. 60) at Anglesey reflects the Jordaens manner. Other seventeenth-century Flemish tapestries in more or less related styles are at Castle Drogo, Cotehele (several sets), Coughton, Lyme, Waddesdon and Powis (where one of the two sets blends particularly happily with the baroque woodwork of the State Bedroom).

A workshop with a large export trade to England was that of Wauters of Antwerp; examples of its work are sets of *Acts of the Apostles* at Great Chalfield Manor, *Playing Boys* at Cotehele, *Tobit* at Hardwick and *Marcus Aurelius* at Packwood. Flemish verdure and landscape tapestries, often with small figures, are at Anglesey, Cotehele, Dyrham, Hardwick, Knole, Lyme, Packwood, Polesden Lacey, Sizergh and Wightwick. Anglesey Abbey also has a Flemish armorial tapestry. The sober magnificence of French seventeenth-century designs affected not only French tapestries such as the *Louis XIV in the Park of Versailles* at Anglesey, but also Flemish work like the *Pyrrhus* set, after

Poussin, at Ham. The coarser style of the Aubusson workshops is well represented by the *Joan of Arc* tapestry at Packwood and other examples at Anglesey, Lytes Cary, Tattershall and Trerice. Towards the end of the period European wars gave rise to a taste for contemporary military subjects, such as the Brussels set of the *Arts of War* at Cliveden; other tapestries of this kind are at Charlecote and Polesden Lacey (pl. 63).

Tapestry was also used to cover seat furniture in the late seventeenth and early eighteenth century; there are examples at Clandon, Waddesdon and the Treasurer's House, York.

In the field of embroidery, a major work of the early seventeenth century is the considerable yardage of silk appliqué, in a strapwork pattern, used for the bed and seat furniture of the Spangle Bedroom at Knole. Other interesting embroideries from that period are cushions at Knole, cushion-covers, pillow-covers and other items at Antony, a pearl-embroidered purse at Fenton and an embroidered book-cover given by Charles I at Ham. Applied needle-work motifs (now mostly reapplied on new grounds) were used to decorate canopies and chairs of the Charles I period at Hardwick, as well as beds at Cotehele and Knole. The chapel at Staunton Harold, built in 1653, retains its original embroidered altar-frontal and other textile furniture; the chapel at Ham also has an original altar-cover. Characteristic embroidered pictures, boxes and mirror-frames worked by young amateur needlewomen of the seventeenth and early eighteenth century, including examples of the raised work known as stumpwork, can be seen at Beningbrough, Cotehele, Fenton and the Treasurer's House, York. Professional raised embroidery in metal thread decorates the King's Bed at Knole and chairs at Hardwick. Crewel-work bed hangings of the later Stuart period, with patterns of leaves and flowers, are at Cotehele, Hardwick, Montacute and Packwood. There are wall hangings with floral embroidered borders at Ham. In the late seventeenth and early eighteenth century applied braids were often used to make formal patterns, as in a bed and a coverlet at Ham and in the state bed and matching window-valances of the early eighteenth century at Dyrham. At Lyme Park a settee of about 1690 is embroidered with vases of flowers, and Clandon has a splendid bed and matching seat furniture with floral needlework of about 1700 (pl. 78). Other furnishing needlework assigned to the late seventeenth or early eighteenth century is at Ascott, Clandon, Packwood, Polesden Lacey, Wightwick and the Treasurer's House, York. Distinguished pieces of Italian embroidery of this period are an altar-frontal and an enormous pictorial wall hanging at Anglesey.

49 *Millefleurs with knight in armour*   Tournai, *c.* 1481   Ht 10 ft, w. 9 ft 2 in.   Montacute House

50 Detail of wall-hanging: octagonal panel
with Mary Queen of Scots' cipher,
monogram and motto, *Sa Vertu Matire*
Oxburgh Hall

51 *Penelope attended by Patience and Perseverance*
English, *c.* 1573   Ht 9 ft 6 in., l. 11 ft 6 in. Hardwick Hall

53 Detail of *Playing Boys* set, from designs by Francis Cleyn   Hatton Garden workshop of ▶
Francis Poyntz, 1679–85   Panel ht 8 ft, l. 11 ft 8 in.   Hardwick Hall

52 Cushion-cover depicting '*The Fancie of the Fowler*'   English, late 16th century   L. 44 in., w. 22 in.   Hardwick Hall

54 Detail from the *Indian Concert*, one of a
set of 'Indian' subjects designed by
John Vanderbank   Soho, 1700–1710
Ht 7 ft 8 in., l. 14 ft 5 in.   The Vyne

55 'April: milking and churning': one of a set of
the *Months*   Mortlake weavers, probably at
Soho, 1699–1719   Ht 9 ft 1 in., w. 7 ft 2 in.
Ham House

56 *Landscape with Figures* designed by John Vanderbank   Soho, *c.* 1720   Ht 7 ft 10 in.,
   w. 16 ft 9 in.   Erddig Park

58 Detail from the Adam Tapestry Room   Gobelins, signed Neilson 1775   Osterley Park   ▶

57 *Diana :* detail from one of the set depicting the story of *Diana and Actaeon*, by François Spierincx
   Flemish, 17th century   Ht 11 ft, l. 17 ft   Knole

59 Detail from *Alexander the Great visits Diogenes*, one of the *Philosophers* series   Mortlake, *c.* 1670
Ht 8 ft 9 in., l. 19 ft   Dyrham Park

60 *Rebecca at the Well*   Bruges, 17th century   Ht 9 ft 9 in., l. 12 ft 6 in.   Anglesey Abbey

61 *America* from the *Continents* set Beauvais, *c.* 1770
Ht 10 ft 2 in., l. 10 ft 3 in. Osterley Park

62 Detail from one of the eight tapestries depicting the
story of Ulysses Brussels, late 16th century
Hardwick Hall

63 Detail of one of the *Camp Scenes*
Brussels, early 18th century
Ht 8 ft 3 in., l. 6 ft 11 in. Polesden Lacey

64 Detail from one of the *Nouvelles Indes* set Gobelins, signed
Neilson 1788 Ht 9 ft 4 in., l. 9 ft 7 in.
Montacute

65 Detail from the screen embroidered by Julia, Lady Calverley, 1727
Screen: ht 8 ft 3 in., l. 12 ft; panels: ht 5 ft 8 in., w. 20 in.   Wallington

The Georgian period

In the lighter, more elegant decorative schemes of Georgian houses, the use of patterned textiles tended gradually to decline. For wall coverings, silk or paper were now generally preferred and tapestries, if used at all, were apt to be confined to a single tapestry room.

English tapestries from the early part of the period, generally attributed to workshops in the Soho area of London, include a set of *Landscapes with Figures* (pl. 56) at Erddig, woven about 1720, a set of *Continents* at Packwood and a tapestry of a *Game of Bowls* at Ascott. An attractive set of Watteau subjects at Ham is signed by Bradshaw and a set of *Hunts* at Clandon is possibly from the same workshop. Also at Clandon is an Arabesque tapestry of the type produced in the workshop of Joshua Morris. Tapestry seat furniture and firescreens, chiefly English, can be seen at Clandon, Antony, Ham and Ascott. Among Brussels tapestries, sets depicting *Peasant Subjects* in the style of Teniers were popular; there are examples at Blickling, Nostell Priory, Polesden Lacey and in the Tapestry Room at West Wycombe Park. The Tapestry Room at Nostell, designed by Adam, has a set of Brussels *Continents*. In the later eighteenth century the changing climate of taste brought tapestry production to an end in Flanders and England, though it continued in France.

The fine collection of French tapestry at Waddesdon includes a screen mounted with *Grotesque Months* after Audran and several sets of eighteenth-century *portières,* as well as a Beauvais set of the *Noble Pastorale* after Boucher. Between the 1760s and the 1780s Gobelins sets of the *Tentures de François Boucher* were ordered for several schemes of decoration undertaken by Adam; a particularly sumptuous ensemble in the Tapestry Room at Osterley, comprising both wall hangings and furniture, is signed by Neilson and dated 1775 (pl. 58). Other sets of French furniture with tapestry covers are at Waddesdon, Petworth, Polesden Lacey and Claydon and there is a fire-screen at Ascott. Also at Osterley is a set of Beauvais *Continents* after Lebarbier (pl. 61), dated 1786. A Gobelins tapestry of the *Nouvelles Indes* set, signed by Neilson and dated 1788, is at Montacute (pl. 64). The coarser tapestries made at Aubusson and Felletin are represented at Anglesey and Polesden Lacey. An unusual tapestry for an English house is that at Blickling depicting *Peter the Great at the Battle of Poltava*; woven at St Petersburg in 1764, it was presented to the Earl of Buckinghamshire by the Empress Catherine.

Among the finest examples of English embroidery from the early eighteenth century are the large hangings depicting garden scenes, which were formerly at Stoke Edith in Herefordshire and are now displayed at Montacute on loan from the Victoria and Albert Museum. Embroidery in knotted thread, a popular technique of the period, is found on early eighteenth-century chairs at Ham and Cotehele. *Gros point* and *petit point* needlework were very extensively used for furnishing purposes, for example in the floral wall panels and pictorial screen panels at Wallington (pl. 65), worked by Julia, Lady Calverley, and dated respectively 1717 and 1727. Sets of chairs with this type of needlework are at Upton, Polesden Lacey, Ascott and elsewhere, while the very extensive collection bequeathed by Mrs Gubbay and exhibited at Clandon includes fine needlework ranging in date from the Queen Anne period to about 1765. Examples of the official, heraldic embroidery of the period can be seen in the state bed at Blickling, the purses of the Lords Privy Seal at Ickworth and other heraldic panels at Anglesey and Polesden Lacey. The state bed at Osterley, with its floral embroidery (pl. 97), was designed by Adam in 1776; in the same room there is an embroidered fire-screen. Other characteristic fire-screens and embroidered pictures of the eighteenth century are at Fenton House. French needlework furniture can be seen at Waddesdon and Polesden Lacey, and there is a great display of Chinese embroidery on the state bed at Erddig.

5

English Furniture

Martin Drury

Taken as a whole the many and varied collections in the care of the National Trust constitute the most important corpus of English furniture in existence, important not only in the sense that implies rarity and good craftsmanship, but because so much of it survives in the setting for which it was intended. To see furniture in this context adds immeasurably to its significance. A humble seventeenth-century table, seen in the room in which it is listed in an inventory drawn up two hundred or more years ago, makes an appeal to the imagination that it could never do in the purely academic context of a museum. At the same time it adds to our understanding of domestic life in a remote period. This enlightening element of continuity is one of the most precious aspects of the English country house and is to be experienced in many of those in the care of the Trust.

Though the range of the Trust's English furniture is wide, the balance is uneven. It is particularly rich, for example, in first-rate furniture of the late seventeenth century, and the principal rooms at Nostell Priory and Stourhead contain a large proportion of the known documented pieces from the workshops of the two Chippendales. By contrast, medieval furniture, of which the few surviving examples are by now mostly to be found in religious buildings, universities and museums, is scarcely represented at all. The Trust's collections also offer relatively few examples of the finest furniture of the Regency period, and few important post-Great Exhibition pieces, whether from the workshops of the early suppliers of the 'mass market' or from the benches of the lone idealists of the Arts and Crafts movement.

Not surprisingly it is in the houses that have enjoyed long continuity of ownership that the oldest furniture has survived. The earliest pieces to which a firm date can be given are a remarkable pair of wrought andirons at Knole. The standards of these strange, gaunt objects carry attenuated human figures and are surmounted by royal crowns. Below the crowns are, on one, the arms of Henry VIII, and, on the other, a falcon crowned, the badge of Anne Boleyn – a heraldic juxtaposition that places them firmly in the years 1533–6. In the late medieval hall at Cotehele, owned by the Mount Edgcumbe family for five hundred years, there is a long table on plain baluster legs (pl. 67) and an oak trestle-bench of joined construction, and in the adjacent Old Dining-Room, a smaller table with deep convex frieze and bulbous baluster legs, heavily charged with gadrooning. Both tables date from the late sixteenth century, by which time it had become customary for the householder and his family to dine apart from their servants, and it is likely that they remain today in the rooms in which they stood in 1580. Two long tables of exceptional size are at Knole and Hardwick. The latter is one of three listed in an inventory of 1601 and the table at Knole is among the few pieces that survived the sale of the contents ordered by Parliament as the price of Lord Dorset's support of Charles I.

Inventories of this period list tables of varying sizes in the principal rooms of great houses. They are usually described as being covered with a carpet or tapestry, but for the more imposing examples increasing use was made of the recently imported technique of inlaying with woods of lighter colour, such as walnut, box and holly. Two such tables survive at Hardwick; the first, nine feet long and inlaid with an elaborate design of musical instruments, playing-boards, cards, an opened book of music and other devices, bears the arms of Hardwick, Cavendish and Talbot, and was probably made in 1568 to mark the almost simultaneous marriages of Bess of Hardwick to her fourth husband, Lord Shrewsbury, and of two of her children to two of his. The second is a square gaming-table, supported by square fluted columns, with a marquetry top inlaid with a design of strapwork and playing cards (pl. 69). Throughout the Middle Ages until well after 1600 the bench was the principal seat used when eating by all but those of high degree and at Sizergh there is an example of trestle form, with traces of Gothic influence in its carved detail. Others in the house, similar and in a better state of preservation, bear the date 1562. If, as seems likely, these are copies of the original, the latter could lay claim to be the earliest piece of furniture in any National Trust house. But it could be that the benches are all of a date and that one received rougher treatment elsewhere in the house before being reunited with its fellows. Also at Sizergh is a massive oak joined dower-chest initialled and dated WS 1571 AS. Walter and Alice Strickland were married in that year.

Before leaving the sixteenth century mention must be made of the terrestrial globe at Petworth, which, though not strictly a piece of furniture, does not fall readily into any other category. It was made in 1592 by Emery Molyneux, the first maker of globes in England, and is believed to be the oldest surviving example of his work. Tradition has it that it was given by Sir Walter Raleigh to the ninth Earl of Northumberland (known as the Wizard Earl for his interest in science and alchemy) when they were fellow prisoners in the Tower.

Dotted along the limestone belt that cuts a swathe diagonally across England

66 James II's bed, c. 1685–8, attrib. Thomas Roberts   W. 78 in., l. 94 in.   Knole

67 Oak refectory table, late 16th century   Ht 31½ in., l. 13 ft 6 in., w. 35 in.   Cotehele

68 Bedroom furniture, 17th century, carved and signed by members of the Browne family
Townend Farm

69 Gaming table, *c.* 1580   Ht 34 in., w. and
   d. 41 in.   Hardwick Hall

70 X-framed State armchair, stamped HC
   (for Hampton Court) 1661   Ht 53 in.,
   w. 32 in., d. 21 in.   Knole

71 Oak bed, early 17th century   Ht 7 ft 5 in., w. 5 ft 9 in., l. 7 ft 5 in.   Montacute

73 Giltwood settee, *c.* 1740, designed by William Kent   Ht 42 in., w. 59 in., d. 27 in.
Ionic Temple, Rievaulx Terrace

◀ 72 Seaweed marquetry looking-glass and table, late 17th century   Mirror: Ht 58 in., w. 33 in.;
table: ht 29 in., w. 37 in., d. 25 in.   Beningbrough Hall

74 Card table in the style of Gerreit Jensen, *c.* 1690   Ht 28½ in., w. 32 in., d. (folded) 10¾ in.
    Clandon Park

75 Writing cabinet or 'scriptor', *c.* 1670   76 Oak glass-fronted bookcase, *c.* 1675
    Ht 54 in., w. 35¼ in., d. 16 in.   Ham House   Ht 54 in., w. 56 in., d. 18 in.   Dyrham Park

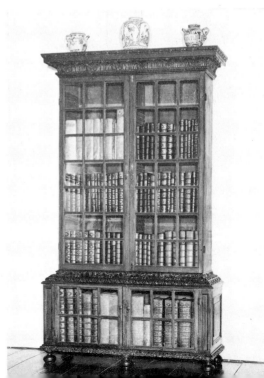

77 State bedroom, *c.* 1660–85: the early 18th-century crimson cut-velvet upholstery and hangings were made at Spitalfields   Powis Castle

78 State bed, with silk embroidery hangings, *c.* 1700   Ht 13 ft 5 in., w. 5 ft 4 in., l. 6 ft 6 in.
Clandon Park

79 Satinwood *bonheur-du-jour, c.* 1774   Ht 40¼ in., w. 27 in., d. 18½ in.   Uppark

80 Walnut settee (from a set of eight chairs and a settee), *c.* 1715–20   Ht 46 in., w. 73⅛ in.,
   d. 37½ in.   Montacute

81 Giltwood side table, early 18th century, by Gumley and Moore   W. 50 in.   Clandon Park

82 and 83 Side table and its design by James Paine, 1750   Ht 2 ft 11 in., w. 6 ft 1 in., d. 3 ft 2 in.
Nostell Priory

84 Side table and torchères, *c.* 1671, attrib. Pierre Golle   Table: ht 33 in., w. 49 in., d. 29 in.; torchères: ht 43½ in.   Knole

85 Writing-table (*bureau plat*) by André Charles Boulle (1642–1732)   Ht 30½ in., w. 71 in., d. 34 in.   Felbrigg Hall

86 Commode by Charles Cressent (1685–1768) Ht 35⅞ in., w. 62¼ in., d. 26 in.
Waddesdon Manor

87 Louis XVI cylinder-top desk (*bureau à cylindre*)
by David Roentgen (1743–1817) Ht 44½ in.,
w. 38½ in., d. 23 in. Anglesey Abbey

88 Writing-table (*table à écrire*),
c. 1780, by Jean-Henri Riesener
Ht 28⅞ in., w. 23¼ in., d. 16½ in.
Waddesdon Manor

89 Serpentine lacquer commode, *c.* 1770,
by Matthew Boulton   Ht 38 in., w. 45 in.,
d. 26½ in.   Polesden Lacey

90 Serpentine commode, 1760–70,
by Pierre Langlois   Ht 33 in., w. 36 in.,
d. 20½ in.   West Wycombe Park

91 Chinese Chippendale cabinet and mirror-picture frames, *c.* 1755, in the Blue Saloon
Shugborough

92 Chair from state bedroom (one of a pair),
   1777, designed by Robert Adam
   Ht 39¾ in., w. 25 in., d. 22 in.
   Osterley Park

93 Mahogany lyre-back library chair
   (one of a set of six), 1767–8,
   by Thomas Chippendale
   Ht 38¼ in., w. 26¾ in., d. 23⅝ in.
   Nostell Priory

94 Drop-front secretaire (*secrétaire à abattant*), *c.* 1745–9, by Jean-Baptiste Tuart
Ht 44 in., w. 24 in., d. 14 in.   Polesden Lacey

95 Satinwood commode (one of a pair), *c.* 1773   Ht 35½ in., w. 62 in., d. 23 in.   Osterley Park

96 Giltwood settee (from the suite of two settees and eighteen armchairs), 1770–71, in the
     Saloon. The damask upholstery is modern   Ht 43 in., w. 104 in., d. 38 in.   Saltram House

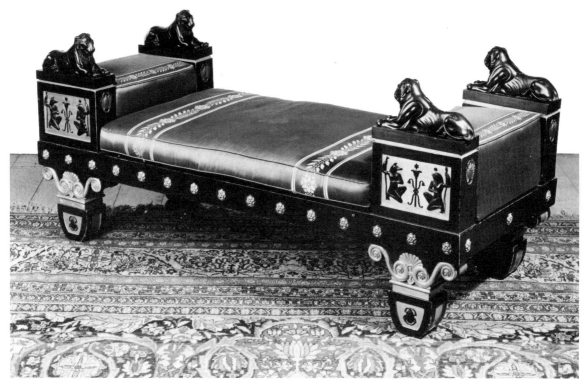

98 Couch or hall settee, 1802, designed by Thomas Hope L. 5 ft 6 in. Buscot Park

◀ 97 State bed, *c.* 1775, designed by Robert Adam Ht 14 ft 7 in., w. 7 ft 2 in., l. 8 ft 4 in.
Osterley Park

99 Mahogany library table, 1805, designed by Thomas Chippendale the Younger
Ht 31¾ in., w. 96 in., d. 45¾ in. Stourhead

100 State bedroom: the oak bed, *c.* 1840, designed by Thomas Hopper   Penrhyn Castle

101 Oak sideboard, 1858,
carved by J. M. Willcox
L. 12 ft.   Charlecote Park

are numerous small manor houses. The restoration of these vernacular build-ings, so long despised as antiquated and uncomfortable, was inspired by the same romantic spirit that gave impetus to the National Trust in its early days. For this reason many, fully restored and refurnished, were among the first acquisitions of the Trust and it is in consequence richer in seventeenth-century oak furniture of provincial origin than in any other field. However, since the craft of furniture-making was still largely unaffected by foreign influence and deeply conservative, variations tend to be in detail rather than type or form. Detailed discussion of them would be beyond the scope of this short chapter. It must be sufficient, therefore, to mention a few representative examples of standard pieces. The long table in oak or elm on turned legs, joined by stretchers, was the principal feature of the hall, still the nucleus and main assembly room of both house and surrounding community. Examples can be seen at Lytes Cary and Great Chalfield (and also at Sizergh, Benthall, and the Treasurer's House, York).

The increasing emphasis on privacy and the emergence of rooms intended solely for the use of the householder's family called for smaller and more adaptable furniture. The folding gateleg table was one such innovation and there are several at Cotehele. At Clevedon Court there is a drawer-leaf table on fat gadrooned legs.

Though the traditional chest remained important and ubiquitous for storage, travelling and sitting upon, it was in the seventeenth century almost always of the panelled type, often enriched with carving, or inlaid. There are examples of both types among the furniture in the Lower Hall at Nostell. This collection is thought to have come from the old Priory, bought by Rowland Winn in 1650 and demolished a century later. The first trunks, in the modern sense, were made towards the middle of the century. They were constructed of deal, covered with leather and studded with brass nails, the angles protected by shaped brass straps, decoratively fretted or engraved. There are splendid examples at Knole and Petworth, and a later one at Hardwick is dated 1727.

In medieval inventories and wills the bed usually appears as the most valuable single item and so it remained throughout the seventeenth century. From the Tudor period, however, the frame gradually assumed greater im-portance. From being a rough-hewn frame intended as the unseen vehicle of rich hangings, it became itself the subject of extravagant decoration with heavily panelled and inlaid backboard and carved tester, often supported by massive turned and carved posts. This form of bed, in which for the first time the hangings played only a functional role, reached its apotheosis in the Jacobean period, as exemplified by a massive specimen at Montacute, which bears the arms of James I, of Henry, Prince of Wales and of Frederick, Elector Palatine, carved in bold relief on its headboard (pl. 71). A rare example, smaller but no less elaborate, is at Great Chalfield.

H*

It was only in the seventeenth century that the chair began to lose its significance as a symbol of authority and the oak armchair with panelled back, solid seat and turned legs and arm supports, became a common feature of houses too numerous to specify. The chair dated 1627 at Cotehele, whose back is pivoted to convert into a table, should be mentioned in passing. Rarer is the chair (or 'backstool'), a development, not of the armchair (or 'chayre'), which has an ancient pedigree, but, as its contemporary name suggests, of the stool. Unknown before the seventeenth century, the 'backstool' (often misleadingly called a farthingale or Cromwellian chair) quickly became the commonest form of seat alongside the stool. Because they were usually of softwood, covered with Turkey-work or finer cloth, only the most splendid examples (and those of oak and leather) have survived.

Ranged along the walls of the Leicester Gallery at Knole are two suites of seat furniture of this type, comprising in all six stools, six backstools and two settees. They retain their original crimson velvet, much decayed, and their exposed frames are gessoed and silvered and decorated with traceried patterns in red and gold. Much of the furniture at Knole is known to have come from the royal palaces of Whitehall and Hampton Court, as this sequence no doubt did, but, whatever its provenance, it constitutes the grandest, perhaps the oldest, set of Jacobean seat furniture in existence. In the same gallery is the famous 'Knole settee'. This venerable object, also of about 1610, is much more than just the progenitor of all upholstered seats large enough to seat more than one person, it is a 'chair of state' that once stood, probably in Whitehall Palace, upon a dais and beneath a canopy or 'cloth of estate', and was a potent symbol of royal power. At Hardwick another such chair can be seen. Shaped like a deep-bottomed punt, with no back, it has fixed end-panels on which can be made out the painted arms of Christian Bruce and her husband, the second Earl of Devonshire, who inherited the house in 1625.

The more familiar form of the chair of state is the X-form, in which both Queen Elizabeth and James I were painted. Of this type no less than five are preserved at Knole, three covered in their original silk or velvet and two stamped with the date 1661 and the inventory mark of Hampton Court Palace (pl. 70). Opinion is divided as to whether they date from c. 1610 or 1660, but there is no doubt that they found their way to Knole as perquisites of the sixth Earl of Dorset, who exercised his right as Lord Chamberlain to William III, to certain state furniture associated with the preceding monarch.

The restoration of Charles II brought a sudden and dramatic change in the development of English furniture. The native styles, which had slowly evolved over two centuries, were overwhelmed by a flood of foreign ideas and techniques. From twenty years of exile on the Continent the Court returned with a taste for luxury and sophistication that could only be satisfied by immigrant craftsmen from France and Holland. Construction became lighter and more elegant; walnut replaced oak as the wood most favoured for the best pieces; the new techniques of veneering, marquetry and japanning superseded carving and inlay for the embellishment of flat surfaces.

Something of the extreme richness that was the keynote of the late seventeenth-century interior can be recaptured today in the splendid though faded interiors of Ham and Knole. The former was fitted up in the most lavish style of the day by the Duke and Duchess of Lauderdale in the 1670s. Much of the original furniture survives in the house and has recently been rearranged by the Victoria and Albert Museum to accord with the still extant inventory of 1679. Here are examples of each of the new techniques and of new types of furniture. The cushion-framed marquetry looking-glass in Lady Maynard's Chamber and the table below it are superb examples of marquetry, a technique newly learned from the Dutch; a similar looking-glass has a frame overlaid with incised sheets of oriental lacquer (known as Coromandel or Bantam work); its companion table and a cabinet on gilded stand are veneered in the same manner; the well known set of 'backstools' were described in 1679 as 'japanned' to indicate that they were of native manufacture, being gessoed, painted and varnished in imitation of Chinese work; there is also a fine lacquer cabinet with raised rather than incised decoration, imported entire from the East and mounted on a gilded stand of Anglo-Dutch design. Of the new types of furniture, perhaps the most notable is 'the scriptore of princewood garnished with silver' (1679 inventory), one of two silver-mounted secretaires in the house (pl. 75), and a fine example of the earliest floor-standing cabinets designed specifically for writing. Looking-glasses themselves were an innovation. Great advances were being made in the manufacture of plate-glass and, though the larger 'Vauxhall' plate was now in production, silvered glass remained an expensive commodity until the end of the eighteenth century. (The polished steel 'speculum' of 1625 at Cotehele, mounted in an ebonized frame, is a rare surviving example of the precursor of the looking-glass).

An innovation of the period that is not to be found at Ham is the glazed moveable bookcase. The first recorded examples are those made between 1666 and 1705 for Samuel Pepys by Christopher Sympson and now at Magdalene College, Cambridge. Thomas Povey, uncle of the builder of Dyrham, was a Caroline man of fashion and a friend of Pepys. Many of his possessions came to Dyrham after his death and it is likely that the tall oak book-press in two tiers (now in the Hall) was amongst them (pl. 76). It is identical to those at Magdalene and was probably supplied by the same maker in about 1675.

The famous group of furniture encased in embossed silver at Knole is discussed elsewhere in this book. It consists of a table, a looking-glass and two candlestands. Such a group, although rarely embellished in silver, was standard equipment in the grandest bedrooms in the late seventeenth century and there is another at Knole, veneered in pearwood and japanned. In this version the looking-glass, recently recovered from the attics, has lost its fragile fretwork cresting. More usually, such groups were veneered in walnut and decorated with marquetry in floral or 'seaweed' designs, but the form varied only slightly: rectangular side-table with one drawer in the frieze, looking-glass with cushion frame and shaped cresting, two stands with hexagonal or circular tops on turned or 'S' stems and tripod feet. There are fine examples at Beningbrough, of a slightly later date (pl. 72). As their original relationship came to be forgotten the components were often separated. There are three tables without their stands and glasses in the State Bedroom at Clandon, while the set veneered in walnut at Dyrham has long since lost its accompanying glass.

The taste for extravagance and display that characterized the late seventeenth century found its most sumptuous expression in the great beds of the Restoration period. Every great house had its State Bedchamber, in theory for the accommodation of the monarch or other guests of high standing, but in fact rarely slept in. As the conventional yardstick by which a man's wealth and standing could be judged, it was furnished more expensively than any other room and the soaring bed with hangings of imported silk or velvet, the frames gilded or covered with stuff, quickly displaced for ever the ponderous, insular wainscot bed of the Montacute type. We must return again to Knole for two of the earliest and most splendid. In the Venetian Ambassador's Bedroom is the bed of James II (pl. 66). Its carved and gilded tester and feet carry his royal cipher and it is hung with green cut Genoa velvet. The bed and its accompanying chairs and stools, all of 1685-8, are attributed on grounds of style to Thomas Roberts, the royal 'joiner' between 1685 and 1714. It is exceeded in magnificence only by the bed in the King's Room, also probably made for James II, but now thought to be of French origin.

After 1690, through the influence of the Huguenot designer Daniel Marot (1663–1752), state beds assumed an elaboration that verged on the fantastic. That at Clandon has silk needlework in an astonishing state of preservation (pl. 78). That at Dyrham also retains its original hangings, here of crimson and yellow velvet, and there are others at Beningbrough, Lyme and Buscot, though the last has lost its original curtains. The distinctive feature of beds of this type is the elaborately shaped but hidden pine headboard and tester, forming a matrix for the draped and bunched textiles, tassels and fringes, which give the design its characteristic flourishes.

In marked contrast to the formal splendour of the State Bedroom, the concept of privacy, unknown in the Middle Ages and not highly valued before 1600, began to find expression in both architecture and furniture. Beyond the public rooms little private chambers or closets were provided for rest, writing, intimate conversation, and card and table games. The 'scriptores' at Ham were each placed in such rooms in 1679 and an example of the first form of table designed for cards can be seen at Clandon (pl. 74). It has retracting legs with gilded Corinthian capitals and a fold-over top. It is veneered in walnut and decorated in the fine 'seaweed' marquetry associated with the royal cabinet-maker Gerreit Jensen (*fl. c.* 1680–1715). Two such pieces dating from about 1710, oval when open and veneered in figured walnut on turned legs linked by stretchers, are now at Beningbrough. Such early card tables are rare. Also at Beningbrough is a table intended specifically for playing piquet.*

After the death of William III in 1702, when French influence went into eclipse, a native style re-emerged. The comfortable, practical and sturdily constructed furniture of the Queen Anne period, expressed in carefully selected veneers of figured walnut, gilded surfaces cut in low relief, some japan and much needlework, was as apt an expression of the English character as the preceding years of display had been a magnificent aberration. The twelve walnut chairs at The Vyne with pierced splats shaped to accommodate the sitter's back, others, in the chapel at Erddig, with splats inset with marquetry, and the comprehensive assembly at Clandon, all comfortably upholstered and covered in contemporary needlework or tapestry, contrast tellingly with the tall-backed, carved and caned specimens of the preceding decades. It is with good reason that the latter have been relegated in so many houses to entrance halls and corridors. Indeed, for comfort the wing chair, of which there are examples covered in needlework, with only the polished walnut of the short cabriole legs exposed, at Clandon and Beningbrough, has never been improved upon. Less comfortable, but compact and now rare, are the two 'shepherd's crook' armchairs (so called from the form of the arms) at Beningbrough, one with veneered back and upholstered drop-in seat, the other with stuffed back and seat. There are two-seater settees at Clandon covered in Mortlake tapestry; and a larger version in parcel-gilt walnut at Montacute (pl. 80). Others at Erddig and Powis have silvered gesso frames and retain their original crimson Spitalfields cut-velvet. The last three mentioned are *en suite* with sets of side-chairs, while the set at Powis also has round stools to match (pl. 77).

The impractical 'scriptore' or *escritoire* now evolved into the bureau-cabinet, which ingeniously combined a bureau with short, sloping fall-front, chest of drawers and bookcase. A handsome version in burr walnut with an arched broken cornice and doors with bevelled mirror-plates is at Beningbrough and there are others at Dyrham and Erdigg. Also at Erddig are two of slightly earlier date, one japanned in black, the other in red They both have double-arched cornices and stand on bun feet. Like all the furniture at Erddig, they are in a remarkable state of preservation. Japanning in the early eighteenth century could employ, in increasing order of rarity, a ground of black, blue,

* Many of the pieces mentioned in the text at Beningbrough and Clandon are from the collections bequeathed to the Trust respectively by Lady Megaw and Mrs David Gubbay.

green, red and ivory. Of the last, the National Trust has no example, but at Clandon there is an unusually small cabinet of about 1710, japanned on a green ground, with giltwood cresting and claw feet. The set of green japanned side-chairs at Erddig with stools to match, on hocked legs with drop-in seats, is of exceptional rarity.

The supreme achievements of this period, and some of the most expensive, were the large gilt or silvered pier-glasses, supplied by London makers, of which the partnership of Gumley and Moore was the best known. Invoices dating from 1720 to 1726 from this firm are preserved at Erddig and most of the glasses to which they refer still hang in the rooms in which they were listed in an inventory of 1733. The most notable are the 'pair of Large looking-glass sconces in carved and gold frames with double glass branches', described in a bill dated September 6th, 1720. Another, dated June 6th, 1726, probably refers to the glass of similar design, but with silvered frame and *en suite* with a pier-table, which has a top of mirror glass, cut, coloured and gilt with the arms of John Mellor. Mellor was a rich London lawyer who furnished Erddig at this time 'in ye grandest manner and after ye newest fashion'. Very little has changed at Erddig since he died in 1735.

There is a gilt gesso pier-table in the house, probably by James Moore, and a finer pair at Clandon (pl. 81). These last have Indian masks on the knees, scaled legs ending in dolphin feet, and the carving in gesso is in exceptionally high relief. Chandeliers were treated in the same manner and there are notable examples of about 1725 at the Treasurer's House and Beningbrough.

By 1710 the chest or coffer was finally replaced by the chest of drawers for the storage of clothes. The chest of drawers took various forms, all of which are simple in design and often veneered with beautifully figured walnut. One form is the tallboy; there is an example with canted and fluted angles to the upper portion at Erddig and another similar at Beningbrough. Another form is the 'bachelor's chest', a low, shallow piece of furniture with a top that folds forward on to retractable bearers, thereby doubling its area and providing a surface for brushing clothes. There is a chest of this type at Beningbrough, and a well known set of four at Stourhead, the drawer-fronts outlined with a light-coloured banding, with chamfered corners. A third form, the chest on stand with three drawers in the stand and on cabriole legs, is also represented at Beningbrough.

In those great Palladian houses whose interiors were decorated by William Kent (1686–1748), furniture formed an integral part of the design, and his side-tables, looking-glasses and seat furniture had in consequence a massive, architectural quality, which Horace Walpole found 'immeasurably ponderous'. The Trust has no house in which Kent had a hand, but in the Ionic Temple that dominates one end of the terrace above the ruins of Rievaulx Abbey, the late Lord Feversham placed a pair of giltwood settees, carved with female masks on the back rails, and pairs of sphinxes on the aprons (pl. 73). They are identical with those designed by Kent for the Double Cube Room at Wilton. Also in the Temple are a pair of eagle console tables in the same manner and above them pier-glasses with swan-necked pediments, divided by masks and scallop shells. Other furniture inspired by the designs of Kent are a settee, table and looking-glass, at Stourhead; a heavily carved writing-table in dark San Domingan mahogany and two marble-topped giltwood side-tables at Clandon; and at Knole a giltwood marble-topped side-table and pedimented looking-glass, both of gargantuan dimensions.

This architectural character predominates in the design of a pair of side-tables in the Dining-Room at Nostell, for which a drawing by the architect James Paine (c. 1716–89) is preserved in the house (pls. 82 and 83), but here something new is also discernible. Garlands of vines and sinuous C and S scrolls lighten the ponderousness to which Walpole objected. As an uneasy synthesis of Kentian and rococo elements, these tables are an appropriate introduction to the great age of inventiveness in English furniture design. The rococo style seeped in slowly from across the Channel during the 1740s, and with the publication of Thomas Chippendale's *Gentleman and Cabinet-maker's Director* in 1754 it was given expression in a wholly original variety of forms. The *Director* was the inspiration of a generation of furniture-makers, but curiously little furniture is known to have been supplied by Chippendale himself in the manner his published designs made popular. Cash payments to his firm are recorded in the account-book preserved at Saltram. In the absence of invoices, one cannot be sure, but the payments probably refer to the giltwood settees and chairs in the Saloon (pl. 96), which are similar to chairs at Harewood known to be by Chippendale. Three card-tables also qualify on grounds of style and workmanship.

The freedom and lightness of rococo design was most effectively realized in the frames of looking-glasses and girandoles, whether in the Chinese taste as at Claydon or the Gothick as at Lyme and Croft. There are no less than eight large pier-glasses at Petworth in the full-blown naturalistic manner of the designer, Thomas Johnson. At Clandon there is a more massive example, incorporating the baldachino fringe, a motif often employed by Matthias Lock (c. 1740–69), a carver already working in the rococo style in the 1740s. At Nostell is the pier-glass 'in a very fine large border'd Chinese frame Richly carv'd and finish'd', invoiced by Chippendale in 1771; and at Uppark there is a series of rococo looking-glasses, of which the finest are the large pair of pier-glasses in the Red Drawing-Room.

Uppark, like Erddig, has survived with its contents almost intact since the eighteenth century. It was furnished by the rich and cultivated Sir Matthew Fetherstonhaugh and his young wife in the early 1750s and, with its faded damask wallpapers, original festoon curtains, Grand Tour pictures and rococo furniture, it is a powerful evocation of mid-eighteenth-century taste. Sir Matthew had his crest incorporated in marquetry on a little *bonheur-du-jour* of about 1774 (pl. 79). Also at Uppark are a pair of *bombé* commodes in the Louis XV manner of about 1765. They are veneered with panels of black Chinese lacquer within japanned borders and have giltwood mounts simulating ormolu. There is a similar, but smaller, pair at Powis and one at Polesden Lacey (pl. 89) with ormolu mounts of unusually high quality for an English commode.

While on the subject of 'chinoiserie', a recurring theme in the decorative arts in England, mention must be made of the unique cabinet on stand at Uppark. This exotic fantasy is japanned and gilded, with fretted galleries and surmounted by three pagoda-roofed pavilions hung with giltwood bells. Florentine *pietre dure* panels are incorporated with ivory cameos of Brutus and Homer, all acquired in Italy by Sir Matthew who no doubt commissioned the cabinet as a vehicle for their display. There are imported Chinese paintings on mirror-glass, mounted in gilded rococo frames, at Saltram and three in fanciful 'chinoiserie' frames at Shugborough (pl. 91).

Of Chippendale's notable contemporaries, the firm of Vile and Cobb supplied furniture to Anthony Chute of The Vyne in 1752–3. Four of the set of 'six neat mahogany chairs, stuffed, in linen', invoiced at 19*s*. each, are in the house today, still in their original loose linen covers embroidered with floral sprays. The same firm repaired the fine Florentine *pietre dure* casket and probably made its richly carved and gilded stand with grinning satyrs' masks at each corner. The Frenchman, Pierre Langlois, who worked in England in the 1760s, specialized in marquetry commodes in the Louis XV manner. A pair at West Wycombe (pl. 90) take us effectively into the era of neo-classicism, for though their outline is curvilinear, they incorporate neo-classical motifs in marquetry —husks, paterae, urns, the anthemion and Pompeian vases.

Three great collections of the early neo-classical period survive in National Trust houses: those at Nostell, Saltram and Osterley. The principal rooms in each of these houses are the work of Robert Adam (1728–92) and his designs for much of the furniture they contain are preserved in the Soane Museum and elsewhere. If Osterley can be said to be the most important illustration of one man's towering contribution to the course of neo-classicism in Europe, Nostell can claim a comparable distinction as the repository of over one hundred pieces of furniture known to be by Chippendale or attributed to him with good reason.

As if to prove that it is never wise to give firm dates to changes in taste, the furniture supplied by Chippendale to Nostell between 1766 and 1776 is in a wide diversity of styles, ranging from the massive mahogany library table with carved architectural decoration in the manner of the 1740s, via a small, lightly-drawn lady's writing-table on tapering cabriole legs, to pier-glasses, tables and chairs (pl. 93) in the up-to-date neo-classical idiom of the 1770s.

His firm also supplied the chopping-block in the kitchen and the beautiful Chinese wallpaper that lines the walls of the State Bedchamber and Dressing-Room, indicating the wide range of the furniture and services it could offer. These last two rooms are among the most exotic in any English country house. Chippendale's elaborate chinoiserie mirror hangs between the windows in the bedroom. All the rest of the furniture – beds, dressing-tables, stools, clothes-press, chairs, sofa and commode – is japanned in green, silver and gold. Together, as the guide-book points out, it comprises 'the most complete and best preserved ensemble of Chippendale furniture in existence'. Paine was responsible for the design of the plasterwork in these two rooms before he was succeeded by Adam as architect in 1765. While Chippendale continued to be called upon for the free-standing furniture in the later rooms at Nostell designed by Adam, pieces which formed part of the architectural scheme, such as pier-tables and glasses, were executed by Adam's own craftsmen.

This pattern was also followed at Osterley, though here Chippendale was not employed, and the free-standing furniture was for the most part supplied by John Linnell (d. 1796). The ice-cold splendour and decorative unity of Adam's interiors at Osterley have been a source of admiration ever since Walpole, who from nearby Twickenham kept a close eye on their progress, described the Drawing-Room as 'worthy of Eve before the Fall'. All the principal furniture remains in the house and can today be seen in the very positions that Adam intended for it. The quality of the craftsmanship at Osterley is everywhere of the highest order, and of this the pair of half-round commodes which stand between the windows in the Drawing-Room is the supreme example (pl. 95). Their graceful design, the precision and delicacy of their marquetry and the fine quality of their ormolu mounts combine to make them two of the most visually satisfying pieces of English furniture ever made. Space permits mention of only two other pieces. Adam's famous bed (pl. 97) harks back in its extravagance to the great confections of the first decade of the century. Its vulgarity, noted by Walpole, is made more marked by contrast with the set of chairs which accompany it (pl. 92). These have carved frames of gilded beechwood and oval backs supported by winged sphinxes. Their generous proportions and simple but imaginative design compare favourably with the best French chairs in the Louis XVI style.

At Saltram Adam's work is confined to three rooms, of which the Saloon and the Dining-Room are unified schemes. The great Saloon with its coved ceiling contains pier-glasses and tables and a set of eighteen giltwood chairs and two settees (pl. 96) combining Louis XV and XVI elements in a wholly satisfactory way that would none the less offend the eye of a Frenchman. There are also four giltwood *torchères* supporting one of the great treasures of the house, the ormolu-mounted blue-john candelabra from the workshop of Matthew Boulton (1728–1802). By contrast with the glitter and grandeur of the Saloon, the adjacent Dining-Room is flat-ceilinged and domestic in scale. A cool and harmonious atmosphere is achieved by the absence of gilding and by painting walls and furniture in the same tones of green and white, relieved only by decorative panels by Zucchi and Angelica Kauffmann. The furniture thus integrated comprises a sideboard curved to fit the bowed projection at one end of the room, a pair of flanking pedestals surmounted by urns, and a pier-table and glass.

Robert Adam's inspiration derived from imperial Rome. The second phase of neo-classicism moved further east and drew upon the repertoire of Greece and Egypt. In English furniture the Regency style, which resulted from the injection of these new ideas, found its most extreme and scholarly expression in the designs of the antiquarian banker, Thomas Hope (1769–1831). At Buscot there can be seen an 'Egyptian' clockcase, a pair of black-and-gilt armchairs and a monumental couch, mounted at its four corners with recumbent lionesses (pl. 98). All these are taken directly from plates in his *Household Furniture and Interior Decoration,* published in 1807. A transitional phase, when the emphasis was still on craftsmanship in wood and on the natural qualities of its figure, is illustrated by the uniquely comprehensive assembly of furniture at Stourhead supplied by the younger Thomas Chippendale (1749–1822) to Sir Richard Colt Hoare between 1795 and 1820. In particular, Chippendale was given overall responsibility for furnishing the new Picture Gallery and Library. In the latter his magnificent mahogany writing-table (pl. 99), supported by terms with the heads of sphinxes and philosophers, is proof of a skill and originality as a designer equal to that of his father.

The National Trust is not yet rich in furniture made since 1820, and, though this survey has inevitably had to pass over a great deal that would deserve attention if space allowed, a handful of houses must be mentioned for the special interest of their collections of nineteenth-century furniture.

The first, Charlecote, came to George Hammond Lucy when he was still a young man, newly married to a rich wife. In 1826 they embarked on the refurbishing of Charlecote in what they conceived to be an Elizabethan manner. It is from the furniture that they bought in pursuit of this aim, some of it new, some old, but none in fact Elizabethan, that the peculiar interest of this house derives (pl. 101). The Hammond Lucys, fired by the legendary association of Charlecote with Shakespeare, were amongst the first collectors of 'antiques' in the modern sense.

Penrhyn Castle, designed by the architect Thomas Hopper between 1827 and 1837, is one of the few buildings where the Norman style was applied to domestic architecture. Hopper was also commissioned to design much of the furniture and, with remarkable originality, produced a whole range of pieces in a neo-Norman manner, carved with the chevron, interlocking arcades of rounded arches and other motifs from twelfth-century architecture. Particularly splendid is the great oak bed slept in by Queen Victoria in 1859 (pl. 100), and another made entirely of slate from quarries near by.

Wightwick and Standen were built in the 1890s, to designs respectively by Edward Ould and Philip Webb. Both architects had close links with the firm of Morris & Co., which in each case was called upon to supply furniture. At Wightwick there are examples of the chairs with rush seat and beechwood frame stained black which Morris & Co. made popular, and there is one to a design by Rossetti. To Standen they supplied mahogany chairs and a settee which are unashamed reproductions of Chippendale designs. Also at Standen is a large oval mahogany table on clustered column legs designed by Webb for a house by Norman Shaw in Swan Walk, Chelsea.

6

French Furniture

Gervase Jackson-Stops and William Rieder

From Renaissance court cupboards to neo-classical *bureaux à cylindre*, by way of solid Boulle desks and delicate rococo *bonheurs du jour*, French furniture in National Trust houses covers almost the whole spectrum of styles from the late sixteenth to the early nineteenth century. Despite fits of insular patriotism, the English have always acknowledged French superiority in matters of taste. 'Paris fashion' was considered the last word in modernity three hundred years ago as much as in our own day, and although in the eighteenth century English craftsmen and furniture-makers developed a wholly individual national style of decoration, their stimulus came often from French *émigré* designers like Gravelot and cabinet-makers like Langlois, while men of taste such as Walpole and Beckford continued to be more tempted by the glittering contents of Daguerre's shop in the Rue Saint-Honoré than by the soberer wares of St Martin's Lane.

There are two distinct periods in which most French furniture reached English houses. Before about 1689, the very rich either brought back with them or ordered from France the occasional (usually exceedingly expensive) item of French furniture simply because carvers or upholsterers in this country did not have the technical ability to produce similar objects, or because such rarities conveyed prestige. This situation largely ended with the Revocation of the Edict of Nantes, which flooded England with skilled Huguenot craftsmen, and with Louis XIV's subsequent wars, which not only decreased the demand for works of art in France but also put a virtual end to intercourse between the two countries until the Peace of Utrecht in 1713. It was not in fact until after the French Revolution that English collectors began to buy French furniture in any quantity again, and when they did so it was not for the same reasons as their great-grandparents. The first attraction was simply the enormous amount of superlative Louis XV and Louis XVI pieces which flooded the market after the systematic sales of the Bourbon collections, and those of many other noble families, often knocked down for derisory sums, or given as lottery prizes. This in turn developed into an appreciation in England of the unsurpassed skill of the best eighteenth-century *ébénistes*—Cressent, Riesener, Roentgen and Weisweiler—not generally recognized in France itself till much later. A pioneer of this, in some ways antiquarian, taste was of course Lord Hertford, the founder of the present Wallace Collection, but it was also dealers like Baldock who helped to make this taste general in the 1830s and 40s, reaching a climax at the end of the nineteenth century. The writings of Sir Francis Watson have done much to illuminate the activities of English collectors in this period.

The National Trust is particularly fortunate in having examples of both these kinds of acquisition: the very rare early pieces bought by figures like Bess of Hardwick in the late sixteenth century, or the Earl of Dorset at Knole in the late seventeenth, along with great nineteenth-century collections, such as the first Marquess of Bristol's at Ickworth, the second Earl of Lichfield's at Shugborough, and above all that at Waddesdon Manor, assembled primarily by Baron Ferdinand de Rothschild from the 1870s until his death in 1898. Waddesdon contains one of the finest collections of French furniture in the world and in this field it overshadows all other houses belonging to the Trust. But as an excellent two-volume catalogue of the Waddesdon furniture by Mr Geoffrey de Bellaigue has recently been published, the present authors have chosen to emphasize less well known pieces at other National Trust properties and to discuss those at Waddesdon in a more summary fashion. In the brief compass available, the subject will be approached chronologically rather than by houses.

There is still too little known about the availability of foreign engravings in the early sixteenth century, and the capabilities of native English craftsmen during that period, to decide whether certain outstanding pieces of carved furniture are actually French, English or Flemish in origin. It is only with the famous 'sea-dog' table (pl. 102) and a massive cabinet, both in the Withdrawing-Room at Hardwick Hall, that firmer ground is reached. Undoubtedly the two finest pieces of Elizabethan furniture to survive in England, both are listed in the inventory of the house in 1601, proving them to have been part of Bess of Hardwick's original acquisitions for the house. Both are also based on the engraved designs of Jacques Androuet du Cerceau, perhaps the most influential of the early *ornemanistes*. The chimaeras (dogs with wings and fishes' tails), which support the table, are so finely carved, and the exuberant Mannerist architecture of the cabinet with its inset oil paintings so well handled, that it is safe to say they could not have been made in this country. Bess of Hardwick's wealth enabled her to buy German marquetry cabinets, tapestries direct from Flemish sources, perhaps even (through her son Henry Cavendish) carpets from Constantinople, so the idea of her importing French furniture for her state rooms at Hardwick is understandable. A two-tiered 'buffet' or side-table with panels of delicately carved military trophies also in the Withdrawing-Room at Hardwick is in the more classical style associated with Jean Goujon, and is probably also of French origin.

It is interesting that after over three hundred years the wheel of taste should have turned full circle, and that French Renaissance art should have again come into fashion with English country-house collectors early in our own century. Alongside the rage for Palissy ware in the early 1900s came a renewal of interest in sixteenth-century French furniture. Good examples of this are tables bought by Mrs Greville for Polesden Lacey and by William Waldorf Astor for Cliveden, whose supports are again based on heavy du Cerceau designs.

The import of French furniture to England during the seventeenth century continued to be an activity confined to the very rich, but practically none of their collections (least of all Charles I's) have had Bess of Hardwick's good fortune in surviving largely intact. The few mid-seventeenth-century pieces now in English country houses were almost all acquired at much later dates. A particularly fine example, whose history also shows the large part played by chance in such acquisitions, is a magnificent ebony cabinet (pl. 104) at Nostell Priory in Yorkshire, with its drawers faced in *pietre dure* on a stand supported by carved ebony negroes. This is likely to be an early work of the cabinet-maker Pierre Golle, made soon after he left the Netherlands to settle in Paris, and before he became 'ébéniste du roi' to Louis XIV, for it answers almost exactly to descriptions of other cabinets in Golle's accounts with various important patrons, including Cardinal Mazarin.* The family papers at Nostell reveal that it came to the house through Sabine Louise d'Hervart, the Swiss-born wife of Sir Rowland Winn, the fifth baronet, and was sent from her family's ancestral home near Vevey in 1780.

From later in Golle's career comes an even more important set of furniture at Knole in Kent. This can be dated to about 1670 and comprises a carved and gilt table, with an ebony top inlaid with pewter and brass, and two stands in the form of carved *putti* bearing the emblems of Summer and Autumn (pl. 84). The set is of the greatest interest since it has real claims to have been a gift from Louis XIV to the third Earl of Dorset. Three times Charles II's Ambassador to France and one of the principal negotiators of the Secret Treaty of Dover, Lord Dorset is recorded in 1669 as having been given the French King's portrait set in diamonds and worth £600, so it is more than likely that this furniture (made by the King's cabinet-maker, and carved at the end of each stretcher on the table with the royal fleur-de-lys) should also have been a gift. Once again the pieces tally closely with descriptions of other items supplied by Golle for the French Crown in the 1670s and 80s.

* Kindly communicated by Professor Th. H. Lunsingh Scheurleer, whose research on the work of Pierre Golle also led to the attribution of the table and stands in the Cartoon Gallery at Knole, discussed in the following paragraph.

The history of the outstanding collection of furniture at Knole is complicated by the fact that many of the finest pieces came originally from the English royal palaces, Windsor, Whitehall and Hampton Court, by virtue of Lord Dorset's position as Lord Chamberlain to William and Mary. Following old established custom, the Lord Chamberlain was entitled to any furniture considered outdated, as well as to the entire contents of the room in which a sovereign had died. The marvellous bed which now stands in the King's Bedchamber at Knole is known to have been brought from Whitehall in February 1694 soon after the death of Queen Mary. The wonderful embroidery of its hangings—solid gold and silver thread on the outside, and with a silver arabesque pattern on cherry-coloured satin within—is typical of the very finest Parisian work of the 1680s, while the two armchairs and six stools (pl. 103), upholstered *en suite*, are carved with *putti* holding emblems of love in an equally unmistakable French vocabulary. The answer to the problem of this bed's history is probably contained in an entry in the Royal Wardrobe accounts for 1686 recording payments to a French upholsterer called Simon Delobel for his journey from Paris to London with a bed, a canopy of state and other furniture, which was laid out in the Banqueting House at Whitehall for James II and his queen, Mary of Modena, to inspect. Although the bed and chairs at Knole do not correspond in every detail with a similar set sold by Delobel to the King for the staggering sum of £1,515, their Parisian origins cannot on technical grounds be doubted, and it seems fair to attribute them to him. Delobel had a few years earlier made Louis XIV's own state bed at Versailles,* and since the destruction of that extraordinary confection, the bed at Knole is perhaps the most potent reminder of life at the Sun King's court that is left to us.

Compared to this magnificent, indeed unique, survivor of the High Baroque, the innumerable Boulle kneehole desks, *de rigueur* in English country houses, seem almost commonplace. Amongst National Trust houses with fine examples are Petworth, Buscot, Felbrigg (pl. 85), Shugborough, Powis, Ickworth and Saltram. Boulle, the technique of tortoiseshell inlaid with brass or pewter called after the celebrated cabinet-maker André Charles Boulle, is notoriously difficult to date since it continued in fashion in France throughout the eighteenth century, and since innumerable excellent copies were also made throughout the nineteenth. An example in the Saloon at Erddig in North Wales is therefore of particular interest since it is documented as being in the house as early as 1726, when it appears in an inventory. Evidently, English gentlemen liked to bring back from their travels abroad a 'rarity' like this for their houses, though they had no idea of providing a suitable French setting for it: the Erddig desk was to share a room with a bed of delicately embroidered Chinese silk and an English gilt pier-glass. A visitor to the house in 1732

---

* Described in detail by Felibien and Piganiol de la Force.

described it admiringly as 'Henry VIII's dressing table',* indicating the kind of reaction the uninitiated then had to furniture that was, by their standards, still wildly unorthodox.

Boulle furniture also played a large part in the more informed nineteenth-century taste for French furniture amongst English country-house owners. A very fine pair of commodes in the Carved Room at Petworth in Sussex are of special importance since they came originally from the collection of William Beckford of Fonthill,† one of the first to make French furniture fashionable again after its long period of neglect in England. The commodes are close to Boulle's own engraved designs and probably date from the very early years of the eighteenth century. Also in Sussex, a set of four pedestals in the Saloon at Uppark stamped by the *maître ébéniste*, Étienne Levasseur (1721–98), are good examples of the continuation of Boulle's techniques very late in the eighteenth century. They were acquired by Sir Harry Fetherstonhaugh, a friend of the Prince Regent's, who shared his love for things French.

One of the most important cabinet-makers in the Louis XV period was the *ébéniste* Charles Cressent (1685–1768). Trained as a sculptor he took particular care over his mounts, for which he designed and made the models, on several occasions encountering trouble with the Guild by employing bronze-makers and gilders on his own premises—a practice specifically prohibited. Several examples of his work are at Waddesdon, including a particularly fine commode of about 1730 (pl. 86). In the bold mounts of *putti* reclining on branches, and emerging from the recesses of the front corners, can be seen the essence of Cressent's sculptural, rococo approach to furniture, while the tripartite division of the front anticipates a later evolution in commodes of the Louis XV and Louis XVI styles.

The development of floral marquetry on French furniture in the middle decades of the eighteenth century has been much discussed; it was certainly one aspect which appealed particularly to the English, as can be seen by the number of London cabinet-makers who adopted it. Many examples of French furniture with this type of decoration are found in National Trust houses, including pieces by Jacques Dubois (*maître* from 1742 until his death in 1763), a striking example of whose work is an unusual combined bookcase, secretaire and cupboard of the mid-1740s at Waddesdon, and Pierre Roussel (*maître* 1745–82), one of the leading *ébénistes* of his time, whose signature appears on an exquisite *bureau de dame* of about 1760, at Ickworth, and on a small commode at Polesden Lacey with the inlaid floral sprays typical of his style.

Also included in the fine collection at Polesden Lacey is a *secretaire à abbatant*

* Richard Loveday, notes on a tour made in 1732, published by the Roxburghe Club, 1890, p. 80.
† The commodes were bought by the second Lord Leconfield at the famous Hamilton Palace sale in 1882.

102 Sea-dog table, design attrib. Jacques Androuet du Cerceau (b. *c.* 1510)   Ht 33½ in.,
l. 58 in., w. 33½ in.   Hardwick Hall

103 Gilt and silver-gilt stool (from the suite of two armchairs and six stools), late 17th century
Ht 18½ in., w. 22½ in., d. 18 in.   Knole

104 Ebony cabinet, late 17th century, attrib. Pierre Golle   Ht 7 ft 3 in., w. 4 ft 7 in., d. 3 ft 2½ in. Nostell Priory

105 Drop-front secretaire, cabinet and clock, *c.* 1770, by René Dubois, his widowed mother and Jean Goyer, the clock attrib. Pierre-Antoine Regnault　Ht 13 ft 5 in., w. 67 in., d. 29½ in. Waddesdon Manor

106 The 'Beaumarchais' desk, *c.* 1777–81   Ht 52 in., w. 83 in., d. 44¼ in.   Waddesdon Manor

107 Drop-front secretaire (*secrétaire à abbatant*), *c.* 1770–74, by Maurice-Bernard Evalde   Ht 53 in., w. 31 in., d. 15 in.   Saltram House

108 Music stand and writing-table, *c.* 1775, by Martin Carlin   Ht 30½ in., w. 18⅛ in., d. 15⅜ in.   Waddesdon Manor

by Jean-Baptiste Tuart *père* (recorded as 'un des fournisseurs de la cour entre 1744 et 1753'), veneered with black-and-gold Chinese lacquer panels and with finely cast and chased ormolu mounts bearing the crowned *C poinçon*, the stamp applied to French bronzes between 1745 and 1749 (pl. 94). Another exquisite black-and-gold lacquer secretaire in the Drawing-Room at Ascott bears the stamps of two well-known cabinet-makers, both of whom evidently played a part in its construction. On the under-edge of the table-top, at the back of the piece, is JOSEPH, the usual stamp of Joseph Baumhauer (a German who is known to have been in Paris by the year of his marriage, 1745), and near by, B. V. R. B., that of the Flemish immigrant, Bernard van Risen Burgh.

During the Louis XVI period, large numbers of German cabinet-makers moved to Paris and certainly the most successful of them (indeed, he has been called the most successful furniture-maker in Europe) was David Roentgen (*maître* 1780–1807). He kept a large workshop in Germany, at Neuwied on the Rhine, and opened an emporium in Paris, soon winning the patronage of Marie Antoinette. In 1779 he was granted the specially created appointment of *Ébéniste-mécanicien du Roi et de la Reine* (reflecting the elaborate mechanical devices fitted into his furniture). A *bureau à cylindre* (pl. 87) at Anglesey Abbey, profusely inlaid with marquetry landscapes and views of Russian towns, was reputedly made by him for Tsar Paul I.

Another German immigrant who fared well was Maurice-Bernard Évalde (*maître* 1765). In 1770 he executed a splendid *cabinet à bijoux* with mounts by Gouthière which Louis XVI had ordered as a present for Marie Antoinette. An excellent example of his work, dating from the same period, is the *secretaire à abattant* (pl. 107), decorated in marquetry with vases of flowers and trophies, at Saltram. François Rübestuck (*maître* 1766–d. 1785), though a lesser light, was an *ébéniste* of high quality and is represented in the Trust by three *secretaires*: at Ascott, Shugborough and Petworth.

A popular type of decoration on French furniture in the second half of the eighteenth century was the application of Sèvres porcelain plaques, and the leading craftsman in this manner was the *ébéniste* Martin Carlin (*maître* 1766–85), also of German origin. He worked principally for the two best-known dealers of the time, Simon-Philippe Poirier and his successor, Dominique Daguerre, often to their designs. His furniture is best studied at Waddesdon where there are altogether seven pieces by him mounted with Sèvres (pl. 108).

Any brief account such as this must necessarily concentrate on central trends and the greatest furniture-makers, but it would be impossible not to mention two extraordinary pieces, neither of which represents any trend at all and both of which were acquired by the redoubtable Baron Ferdinand de Rothschild for Waddesdon. Probably the largest piece of French furniture in England (nearly 14 feet in height), if not the most aesthetically successful, is the combined drop-front secretaire, cabinet and clock (pl. 105) of about 1770 stamped by Dubois (in

I

this case indicating manufacture by Jacques Dubois's widow assisted by their son René) and Jean Goyer (*maître* 1760). Although previously thought to have been made for Catherine the Great, this is now in doubt. De Bellaigue summarizes its eccentricity and elusiveness: 'While the character of the individual elements which make up this monumental piece of furniture is typically French, its general appearance is totally foreign to French eighteenth-century taste and it was probably specially commissioned for export. It may well have been designed by a foreign architect or decorator. It is indeed highly improbable that an *ébéniste* would ever have been entrusted with the design of such an unconventional piece of furniture.' Baron Ferdinand purchased it from the Hon. George Fitzwilliam, owner of Milton Hall, Northamptonshire, for whom he promptly had a copy made to replace the original.

The cylinder-top desk (pl. 106) of *c.* 1777–81 at Waddesdon, traditionally thought to have belonged to that man of all talents, Caron de Beaumarchais (1732–99), was offered as a prize in the Paris *Loterie Royale* of 1831 and was described in 1854 as 'the finest piece of furniture in Europe'. Lavishly decorated with ormolu and marquetry (there are ruin scenes derived from compositions of G. P. Pannini, and emblematic marquetry panels after Jacques de Lajoue and C.-N. Cochin), this large and mechanically complicated desk must have been produced by a team of artists and craftsmen, with the overall design probably provided by an architect or decorator. It previously belonged to the sixth Duke of Buccleuch, who fortunately did not request a copy when he sold it to the Baron.

Of Louis XVI furniture, there is an *embarras de richesses* in National Trust houses. Waddesdon is predictably to the fore with furniture by Adam Weisweiler (*maître* 1778–1820) and, perhaps the greatest of all Parisian *ébénistes* working in the second half of the eighteenth century, Jean-Henri Riesener (*maître* 1768–1820). There are no less than eleven pieces by Riesener at Waddesdon, including works made especially for Louis XVI and Marie Antoinette. Outstanding from a historical point of view are the brilliant drop-front secretaire and its companion table delivered to the King's private study in the Petit Trianon in 1777. But perhaps his greatest masterpiece is the little writing-table (pl. 88) made for the Queen between 1780 and 1785, its bronze mounts and panels of marquetry jewel-like in both quality and execution. Riesener is also represented in other Trust houses, with a cylinder writing-table at Ascott and a splendid *secretaire à abattant* at Shugborough, both of which aptly illustrate his style and quality.

The art of the *ébéniste* tended to outshine that of the *menuisier*, or chair-carver, in the second half of the eighteenth century. The Trust, however, has many excellent examples of the latter's work, perhaps the most notable being a very fine suite in the Saloon at Buscot consisting of a settee and chairs stamped by P. A. Bellangé (b. 1757). Upholstered in a typical Napoleonic silk, these are surprisingly harmonious with the English Regency library table, Adam ceiling and the 'Sleeping Beauty' series of paintings by Burne-Jones. The side tables in the Hall at Buscot are also good examples of French Empire craftsmanship. As was shown in the Council of Europe *Age of Neoclassicism* exhibition in 1972, French and Italian Empire furniture was often stylistically closely related. In Trust houses, this is best seen at Attingham Park, where French pieces, such as a fine ormolu-mounted *lit bateau* and a dressing-table with mirror, in the late Lady Berwick's apartments, can be compared with superb Neapolitan white-and-gilt seat furniture, in the Drawing-Room and Picture Gallery. This huge set was acquired by the third Lord Berwick while Ambassador in Naples, and it is thought to have been made for Napoleon's sister, Caroline Murat.

French furniture in the National Trust's collections does not of course stop at Empire pieces. Practically every English country house has its mid-nineteenth-century *bureau-plat* in the neo-rococo style, its Boulle display cases in the china room, and its heavy *armoire*, the last relegated perhaps from the best bedroom to the gun-room by a later generation brought up instead to appreciate Mrs Maugham's delicate painted furniture. Nevertheless, the range of quality as well as style in these French nineteenth-century pieces gives a clearer idea than any museum could of the catholic tastes and enthusiasms of the Victorian collector. With a rarely erring eye, his achievement was to bring together works of art from every century and country, uniting them in comfortable and informal surroundings.

7

European Pottery and Porcelain

Geoffrey Wills

If space permitted, it would be possible to write a history of the majority of makers of European pottery and porcelain, illustrating it with examples of their work owned by the National Trust. Here it is feasible only to describe and depict a representative selection of pieces in Trust ownership.

Pottery

The cradle of European pottery was Italy, where the maiolica made from the fifteenth century onwards acquired a reputation it has never lost. The process of making it involved forming an article in clay, then coating it with an opaque white glaze containing tin on which painting in colours could be executed. Firing in a kiln gave a permanence to the work that was unattainable with oil-painting. Numerous centres for producing the ware were established in Italy, each of them having its attributes which scholars have tabulated so that identification is usually possible. As with all kinds of works of art, however, there will always be examples defying classification and requiring use of a question-mark.

At Polesden Lacey there is a small collection of Italian maiolica that includes a number of plates and dishes as well as some rare figures of birds. A dish on a low foot is painted with *The Judgment of Paris* (pl. 111) with a riverside town providing a background to the scene. It was produced at Castel Durante, near Urbino, and is probably the work of an artist who executed a series of dishes inscribed 'In Castel Durante' and with dates between 1524 and 1526.

Knowledge of maiolica-making extended gradually throughout Europe. Antwerp duly became an important potting centre, with a proportion of its output crossing the English Channel to find a place in British homes. Among such pieces were the floor-tiles in the Chapel at The Vyne, which was built in 1518–27; they are attributed to an Italian working at Antwerp. He was probably Guido di Savini, known as Guido Andries, who left Urbino in the early

109 Vase painted with the arms of William and Mary, by Adriansz Cocks   Delft, late 17th
century   Tin-glazed earthenware, ht 22½ in.   Erddig Park

115 Parrot Eating a Nut   Bow, *c.* 1760   Porcelain, ht 7 in.   Clandon Park

116 The Fortune-Teller Group, by the 'Muses Modeller'   Bow, 1752   Porcelain, ht 7¾ in.   ▶
Wallington

117 Teapot and cover with stand, painted in green and black in the London studio of James Giles Worcester, *c.* 1771 Porcelain, w. of stand 7 in. Saltram House

119 'The Music Lesson'   Chelsea, marked with an anchor in gold, *c.* 1765
Porcelain, ht 15 in.   Upton House

120 Part of Wedgwood dinner service   Queensware, 1795   Wallington

121 Sauce tureen   Wedgwood, 1774   Queensware, w. 7¾ in.   Shugborough

122 Drunken Fisherman (left),
Fisherman with Net (right)
Chelsea, one marked with an
anchor in red, *c.* 1765
Porcelain, ht 7½ in.
Saltram House

123 Pair of sauce tureens, covers
and stands   Chelsea,
c. 1755   Porcelain, w. 11 in.
Erddig Park

124 and 125 *Lucinda* (l.) and *Octavio* (r.), from the Commedia dell'Arte series, modelled by Bustelli, Nymphenburg, *c.* 1760   Porcelain, ht 7½ in.   Clandon Park

126 Scent bottle, Chelsea, *c.* 1755   Porcelain, ht 3½ in.   Fenton House

127 Lady in a Hooped Skirt, modelled by Kändler, Meissen, *c.* 1750 Porcelain, ht 11½ in. Fenton House

128 'Etruscan' vase by Wedgwood
and Bentley   Staffordshire,
c. 1770–75   Basalte ware,
ht 9½ in.   Saltram House

129 'The Father's Darling'
Spill-vase (one of a pair)
Worcester, factory of Barr,
Flight and Barr, *c.* 1810
Porcelain, ht 5 in.
Stourhead

130 Fan-shaped jardinière and stand (*vase hollandais*)   Sèvres, 1758   Porcelain, ht 8½ in.
Waddesdon Manor

131 Vaisseau-à-mât   Sèvres, 1761   132 Beaker and cover   Meissen, *c.* 1730–35
Porcelain, ht 14¾ in.   Waddesdon Manor   Porcelain, ht 5¾ in. Wallington

1500s. One of the Vyne tiles bears an identifiable portrait of Federigo da Montefeltro, Duke of Urbino, who died in 1482.

At the close of the sixteenth century the Antwerp maiolica potters migrated northwards, and in due course the town of Delft became the site of numerous potteries to the products of which it gave its name. Again, much of the output was exported to England, where its decoration blending oriental and Western motifs was as well received as it was elsewhere in Europe. The Delft potters also made straightforward copies of the Chinese porcelain brought to Rotterdam by the Netherlands East India Company; their versions of blue-and-white wares ('Nankin') being greatly admired and sometimes so like the originals as to deceive the eye at a short distance.

At Dyrham and Uppark are to be seen some of the magnificent vases made at Delft for the effective display of the favourite flower of the period, the tulip. Standing up to four feet in height and constructed in sections, they exhibit the dexterity of both potter and painter. Of comparable type to the foregoing is a large urn-shaped vase at Erddig (pl. 109), which can be traced back to 1695. Undoubtedly it was one of a series supplied in that year to Queen Mary for use at Hampton Court Palace. Like some tulip-vases remaining at Hampton, the Erddig piece bears the royal coat-of-arms, the cipher of William and Mary and the monogram of the potter, Adriansz Cocks of Delft. How this vase became separated from the others is unknown, although a family tradition suggests that it was a gift from Queen Anne and came to Erddig through a marriage.

Not all Delftware was on the massive scale of the preceding examples. In complete contrast to them is a pair of small tea-pots at Wallington (pl. 114). Each of them is a close copy of a Chinese wine-pot with a vertical handle, painted in red and blue with flowers and insects in the style of the original. They date from 1680–90, when most tea-pots came from the Far East along with the tea to brew in them, and are among the rarities of Delft pottery.

One of two Antwerp potters who came to England in about 1567 was named Jasper Andries, presumably a relative of the Guido Andries mentioned above. These men were responsible for introducing to the country the making of maiolica: usually referred to in England as tin-glazed earthenware or delft, the latter spelt with a small 'd' to distinguish it from the Dutch product, and in France termed *faience*. Such ware was made in England throughout the seventeenth and eighteenth centuries, with potteries located in London, Liverpool and Bristol. A fine charger at Cotehele House is painted with the armorial bearings of the Company of Weavers (pl. 112), whose crest and arms feature a leopard's head with a shuttle in its mouth. The piece is dated 1670 and is attributed to one of the London potteries.

Probably made at Liverpool were two punch-bowls at Wallington. Each is inscribed LETT US DRINK SUCCESS TO BLACKETT AND FENWICK, an allusion to the election of 1741 at which Sir Walter Blackett, the then owner of Wallington, was a candidate. The toast on the bowls was evidently heeded, as both men were elected.

The French persevered in perfecting *faience*, improving not only the range of shapes but the quality of the decoration. An example is the Marseilles dinner-service at Saltram House (pl. 113) of which each piece is painted in green monochrome with floral ornament centred in the crest of the Parkers, Earls of Morley. The service dates from the third quarter of the eighteenth century.

In addition to delftware there was a very hard variety of pottery known as stoneware, and red and white clays were used for making comparatively coarse articles. In England, potteries making the latter were mainly to be found in Staffordshire where the necessary materials, and the coal with which to fire them, were available in plenty. There are good examples of mid-eighteenth-century stoneware at Clandon; they were glazed by throwing a quantity of common salt into the kiln when it was at its highest temperature, and the product is referred to as saltglazed stoneware. The sophisticated exterior of Waddesdon Manor surprisingly conceals a number of late-seventeenth- and early-eighteenth-century red clay pieces. Typical of them is a charger decorated with a boldly drawn full-length figure of the Duke of York, later King James II (pl. 110). It is signed by its maker, Thomas Toft, who was one of a number of Staffordshire potters using the slip-decorating technique. In this, semi-liquid clay, known as slip, is applied to an article to ornament it in the same manner as icing a cake.

Continually improved methods and purer clays and glazes were used by a number of Staffordshire men, notably Thomas Whieldon and Ralph Wood whose colour-glazed figures are landmarks in progress. Above all, Josiah Wedgwood was able to produce a cream-coloured earthenware in about 1763, which proved acceptable to all and following approval by Queen Charlotte was named Queensware.

Early examples of Queensware in the shape of vases are at Saltram House, while at Wallington is part of a dinner-service given by Josiah Wedgwood to his friend, the Reverend George Trevelyan (pl. 120). At Shugborough there is a sauce-tureen (pl. 121) from the service that was one of Wedgwood's commercial triumphs: the service supplied in 1774 to the Empress Catherine of Russia. Each of the 900-odd pieces is painted with an English scene, every one different, the dish under discussion appropriately depicting Shugborough.

Josiah Wedgwood also experimented to improve stoneware, with the result that in about 1766 he had perfected a hard black material. Because of its resemblance to the natural stone basalt, he named it 'basaltes', and it is of this that several vases at Saltram House are made (pl. 128). The painting on some of them was termed by Wedgwood 'encaustic', although this actually refers to an ancient method by which coloured waxes were melted into a wood panel; a difference in meaning that can confuse.

A visit to Clevedon Court leapfrogs time and brings the survey into the present century. In the old house may be seen representative examples of the work of the Sunflower Pottery, started and directed by Sir Edmund Elton and operated between 1880 and 1920. The shapes and colours of the pottery evoke those decades and are mainly in the *art nouveau* style, 'by turns exuberant, self-confident, sombre, bizarre'.

Porcelain

Two natural materials, china stone and china clay, when fused by heat form porcelain; a fact known to the Chinese for many centuries. The secret was discovered and successfully applied at Meissen, near Dresden, where a factory for porcelain manufacture was established in 1710 by Augustus the Strong, Elector of Saxony. Of the earlier wares there are at Wallington two covered beakers of *c.* 1730–5 (pl. 132) and part of a tea and coffee service painted with flowers and insects of about 1745.

By the middle of the century the modeller Johann Joachim Kändler had created some of his most celebrated figures and groups: animals, birds and, above all, realistic and satirized humans. In this last category his representations of Harlequin are probably the most highly esteemed: dressed in motley, the well-known pantomime character, who originated in the Italian Comedy, is to be seen in several poses at Fenton House. There, too, is Kändler's figure of a lady wearing a crinoline and holding a pet dog, another peeping from beneath her skirt, which was modelled in 1744 (pl. 127).

Despite precautions taken in order to prevent such occurrences, some of the workers left Meissen, taking with them secrets which they used in assisting the establishment of factories elsewhere. There was keen competition for their services, the various rulers of the German states concurring with the view expressed by Duke Charles Eugene of Ludwigsburg that a porcelain factory was 'necessary to the splendour and dignity' of his domain.

Again, at Fenton House is to be seen an array of the productions of most of the German concerns, Fulda, Höchst and others, inspired directly or indirectly by Meissen. A further wide selection is at Clandon Park, where there are three of the Italian Comedy figures (pls. 124, 125) distinctively modelled at the Bavarian Nymphenburg factory by the Swiss-born Franz Anton Bustelli.

With the capture of Dresden by Frederick the Great during the Seven Years War, Meissen lost its place as the most prominent factory in Europe, and was quickly supplanted by Sèvres. The French had commenced production at Vincennes, near Paris, in 1745, following some years of experiment. As it had proved impossible to find suitable clay and stone in the country, recourse was had to an opaque, glass-like mixture that formed an artificial porcelain. In 1756 the concern was removed to Sèvres, between Paris and Versailles, and soon afterwards it was bought by Louis XV, to become known as the Royal Manufactory.

The Trust is most fortunate to possess the magnificent collection of Sèvres at Waddesdon, formed during the nineteenth century by successive generations of the Rothschild family. It includes no fewer than three examples of the vase *vaisseau-à-mât,* of which only eleven examples are known to exist. The vase illustrated (pl. 131) is unique in that its base differs in design from any other, and instead of being scrolled and rococo it is restrained and comparatively severe. Dated 1761, the piece has been described as 'one of the earliest manifestations of neo-classical influence at Sèvres'.

There is more Sèvres to be seen at Upton House, where there are pieces showing the variety of coloured grounds for which the factory gained renown. A pair of vases of the shape known as *vase hollandais,* decorated with panels in colours reserved on a ground of dark blue with a marbled pattern in gold is very similar to one at Waddesdon (pl. 130). Among the smaller examples is a cup and saucer from a service ordered by Catherine of Russia in 1778, four years after the completion of the very different service supplied by Josiah Wedgwood.

Not surprisingly the houses in the care of the Trust are richest in English porcelain, and there are good examples from the major factories as well as from most of the minor ones. In some instances the pieces were purchased in the eighteenth century and have been in the same mansion since the day they were delivered; they were collected at various periods by sufferers from 'china mania'. Numbered among these was Horace Walpole, of whom it was said:

China's the passion of his soul:
A cup, a plate, a dish, a bowl,
Can kindle wishes in his breast,
Inflame with joy, or break his rest.

Chelsea, then on the outskirts of London, was the site of the first important English porcelain factory. Founded in 1745, it followed the example of Sèvres in making an artificial porcelain. Unlike the French concern, and most other establishments on the mainland of Europe, it did not enjoy royal patronage, although it is thought that the Duke of Cumberland, son of George II, offered encouragement.

From the early 1750s Chelsea produced figures and groups in imitation of those being imported from Meissen. Although the originals were usually copied as closely as possible, the different kind of porcelain used by each factory affected the result. The clay/stone Meissen composition, known as 'hard

paste', made a material with which the glaze combined and the colours remained largely on the surface. On the other hand, the artificial glass/clay 'soft
paste' had a glaze that remained distinct from the body, and which tended to
absorb the colours, resulting in a smooth surface and an overall softness of
appearance.

At Upton House there is a collection of Chelsea demonstrating both the
beauty of the porcelain and the virtuosity of those who modelled and painted it.
Early examples include 'Lovers with a birdcage', who are posed at the foot of a
tree, raised on a base strewn with flowers, and datable to about 1755. It bears
the mark of an anchor in red, which was in use between about 1752 and 1756.
Of similar date is a striking pair of figures of fishermen (pl. 122), at Saltram, one
of which is marked with a red anchor. They are such good copies of Kändler's
original models that they were once thought to have been made at Meissen.

Other groups at Upton date from the years 1759–69, when a gold anchor was
used as the factory mark, and despite the onset of the neo-classical style from
about 1760 the bases of these pieces are in the full rococo manner. Typical of
Chelsea at its most exuberant is the large group at Upton entitled 'The Music
Lesson' (pl. 119) which was modelled from a print entitled '*L'agréable leçon*'
engraved by Robert Gaillard after a painting by Boucher. Among other
important examples at Upton are a pair of equally ornate groups depicting two
of the Labours of Hercules, and a rare set of figures of Apollo and the Nine
Muses.

There are also some important examples of Chelsea at Fenton. In contrast
to two figures of a shepherd and shepherdess standing some eleven inches
in height is a collection of the pocket-size 'Toys' for which the factory is
famous. They take the form of scent-bottles (pl. 126) and other trifles, beautifully modelled and decorated, some of them inscribed with amorous mottoes
in French suggesting that they were lovers' gifts.

As well known as the foregoing are the Chelsea tureens in the shapes of
animals, birds and fishes, of which the last are the most uncommon of a generally rare series. At Erddig is a pair of such tureens realistically modelled and
painted as plaice, with the added distinction of being complete with their under-
dishes. They are the only complete pair so far recorded (pl. 123).

The Bow factory was sited on the opposite side of London from Chelsea. It
was probably started in 1744, and, like Chelsea and the majority of other
English factories, made an artificial porcelain. The output comprised a variety
of figures and groups, as well as a good proportion of domestic wares. At
Upton are two figures of *c.* 1750 depicting well known stage performers of the
time, while the pair of parrots (pl. 115) at Clandon are among a number of
other Bow pieces in the house. At Fenton is a pair of tall figures of a man and a
woman, symbolic of Summer and Autumn, which rival Chelsea in their
brilliant colours and gilding.

K

Meissen provided inspiration for figures at Bow no less than it did elsewhere, but the factory had at least one anonymous modeller who did original work. Because of some easily recognizable Muses he has earned himself the name of 'Muses Modeller', and some of his work is at Wallington (pl. 116). His figures and groups are sometimes in the white and sometimes painted sparsely, but in either instance have a charm that is not lessened by the fact that both his men and his women exhibit receding chins and vacant expressions.

At Worcester a porcelain-works was established in 1751, producing well finished wares that frequently owed more to Sèvres than Meissen. The coloured grounds of the former were imitated, and the Worcester porcelain of the 1770s has consistently been esteemed. The apple-green, claret, yellow and other grounds were inset with shaped panels painted with exotic pheasant-like birds, groups of flowers and, occasionally, with human figures. Above all, the gilding framing the panels and covering the rims of dishes and other pieces was applied unsparingly and with delicacy (pl. 118).

Representative of the type are some pieces at Fenton, of which the rarest is a tall, covered vase painted with alternate panels of oriental figures and pink scale pattern. In a completely different style is a tea and coffee service at Saltram, painted in green and black with figures posed among ruins and other buildings (pl. 117). It was almost certainly decorated in the London studio of James Giles, who is known to have bought Worcester porcelain from the makers and painted it in styles to suit his clients.

The complete change that took place after the close of the eighteenth century is visible in the shapes and decoration of porcelain no less than in other objects of art and furnishings. A pair of spill-vases at Stourhead (pl. 129) is akin to much other ware of the early decades of the nineteenth century, when there was an emphasis on very careful painting, heavy gilding and severity of outline. Beneath each vase is inscribed and impressed the maker's mark of Barr, Flight & Barr, Worcester, and the titles of the subjects are added: 'The Mother's Hope' and 'The Father's Darling'. The originals were painted by Adam Buck, who executed other sentimental pictures of children with and without their doting parents.

As the century progressed, the manufacture of porcelain became increasingly industrialized, so that only rarely does there appear any trace of the individuality that gave earlier examples, such as those illustrated here from National Trust houses, their strong appeal.

8

Porcelain from China and Japan

David Sanctuary Howard

The porcelain exported from China to Europe was as anonymous as it was famous. Its place of origin was known but not its makers. It fell demurely into its dynasties and periods – Tang, Sung and Ming; K'ang Hsi, Yung Chêng and Ch'ien Lung; but there was no Michelangelo, no Rembrandt of this oriental porcelain, no Paul Lamerie, no Chippendale, no Kändler. Yet the unnumbered anonymous Chinese potters who fashioned and painted it have left products which will outlive almost any other form of decorative art.

By 1800 England had dominated the trade routes to China for rather less than a century but her East India Company was the largest trading empire that the world had known. This dominance witnessed both the zenith of Chinese skill in making and decorating porcelain, and the destruction by over-stimulation of the Chinese genius for taste and quality. By the time that the factories of Europe, from Dresden to 'The Potteries' could supply the needs of Europe, the potters of Ching-tê Chên had prostituted their art to satisfy an undiscriminating mass-market. This city in Kiangsi Province, close to a range of hills called Kaoling, was said by the Jesuit missionary Père d'Entrecolles in a letter to his superiors in 1712 to 'have three thousand kilns ... and a million souls'. Chinese merchants travelled the six hundred miles north-westwards from Canton every year to buy the porcelain for their foreign customers who required it to be both in the latest taste and, latterly, to reflect European influence to an increasing degree.

By 1560 the Portuguese carracks from Macao were carrying cargoes of Ming blue-and-white porcelain and a steady flow of styles thereafter. In the later seventeenth century the Dutch dominated the trade with Japan and brought blue, red and gold Imari porcelain and Arita ware which were both made in the Arita district of Japan and exported from the port of Imari. The cabinets and walls of Amsterdam also found room for the great Chinese dishes, painted in the early eighteenth century with translucent enamels of which the principal of a limited number of colours was green and which were later to be called *famille verte*. The Honourable East India Company was omnivorous in its demands for Chinese porcelain. In 1733 the cargoes of the *Grafton* and *Harrison* alone included a quarter of a million pieces. By that time many of the wares were painted in rich opaque enamels as varied as the rainbow, but with a dominance of pink so that the whole range was later called *famille rose*.

From the coming of the Portuguese to the middle of the nineteenth century all the European companies had bought wares specially manufactured for them and the term 'antique' as we understand it today was unknown. European taste was modified by each new cargo from the East with its latest decorations. Throughout the long reign of the great Emperor K'ang Hsi (1660–1722) and his son Yung Chêng (1723–35) the Chinese dominated the selection of styles, although they kept a watchful eye on the latest shapes and decorations from Europe (often in other media) and they listened to the Jesuit missionaries who spasmodically had considerable influence at Court. It was not until Ch'ien Lung's reign (1736–95) that Chinese decoration and form – to their eventual downfall – gradually gave way to echoes of Meissen and Chelsea, Worcester and Wedgwood.

It was only in the second half of the nineteenth century that Chinese porcelain of the earlier dynasties arrived in Europe in any quantity, and considerable impetus was given to this by the sacking of the Summer Palace by European troops under Colonel Gordon ('Chinese Gordon') during the T'ai P'ing Rebellion, which was crushed in 1864. Soon after, in the 1870s, the Victoria and Albert Museum and the British Museum started to build their commanding lead in porcelain, largely through the generosity of such bequests as those of Salting and Franks. In the twentieth century a third museum of comparable importance has come into existence, for the collections which are now in the houses of the National Trust form an 'open museum', complementing and completing the older museums in the way that the Open University complements the established universities.

The Trust has this great advantage: it can display a service of porcelain in the way it was intended and in the surroundings for which it was made. One has only to think of the great displays of armorial porcelain at Ickworth or Shugborough to savour the splendour of dining from such ware. One can feel the pleasure of Elihu Yale at Erddig, the Stricklands at Sizergh and the Parkers at Long Melford, when the wares of China they had bought, been given by kings, or plundered from Spanish vessels were first displayed in the homes where they still remain. One can appreciate the satisfaction of the Trevelyans when the dowry of Chinese porcelain which was the portion of Maria Wilson, later Lady Trevelyan, arrived at Wallington; and the pride of the Winns when the largest of all known armorial dinner-services for the British market – over six hundred pieces heavily decorated in gold and sepia – found its way to Nostell.

Perhaps the earliest piece of Chinese porcelain with a continuous documented history in England is the early sixteenth-century celadon bowl (with its mount of about 1530) given by Archbishop Warham to New College, Oxford, in 1532. Lord Treasurer Burghley, who is twice recorded as having given 'purselyn' to Queen Elizabeth, had made a collection at Burghley House of Ming porcelain with silver and gilt mounts which was dispersed in 1888. In 1953 a piece from this collection – a coffee-coloured upright tea-pot, with charming white slip-ware chrysanthemums, and later silver gilt mounts (possibly made in Augsburg, without any date or mark visible) – was acquired by Lord Fairhaven for Anglesey Abbey (pl. 135), where it now competes with a number of other very individual pieces of later Chinese craftsmanship, including a pair of exceptionally beautiful powder-blue vases of about 1730, mounted in typically heavy Louis XV ormolu as ewers.

On April 2nd, 1682, Elihu Yale, whose name will ever be associated with the small Connecticut college which he partially endowed, wrote from Fort St George in India to Joshua Edisbury at Erddig: 'I begg you and your Ladyes acceptance in part of one of the vessells fill'd with our best Mango Atchar to yourself and to her a Japan Skreene which come upon the ship Bengall Merchant.' The screen *was* accepted and is still at Erddig, the mango atchar was long since eaten, but the *famille verte* porcelain jars here are probably part of the cargo which Yale brought with him to England on his return in 1699 for, contrary to belief, the mango vessels would not have been of a quality to display. Erddig, with its porcelain, its Chinese silks and wallpapers, is among the earliest spiritual homes in England of the Chinese taste.

By the time the East India Company had established their first 'factory' (warehouse) at Canton in 1715, the Strickland family and their direct ancestors had already lived for five centuries at Sizergh Castle in Cumbria, where they still live today. The family remained staunchly Catholic through the unhappy strife of the late seventeenth and early eighteenth century. Sir Thomas Strickland and his cousin Richard of Catterick were the Treasurer and Receiver-General of the exiled Mary of Modena, wife of James II, at St Germain, while Richard Strickland's daughter, Theresa, was her lady-in-waiting. The Queen gave Theresa a fine Japanese bowl of Kutani ware of the late seventeenth century, imported through Holland, mounted in silver with a decorative motif which was itself to become a border pattern on the Chinese porcelain of about 1720 (pl. 144). There are other smaller pieces of the same ware and almost certainly the same provenance and all now rest in the top floor of the Pele Tower, built in 1350. There are also at Sizergh two pairs of massive eighteenth-century fish-bowls and perhaps the last remaining armorial plate from a service made about 1780 for the Hornyold family, ancestors of the present branch of the Strickland family.

An armorial service of oriental porcelain was a hallmark of a taste for chinoiserie in the eighteenth century. Some four thousand were made for

British families, perhaps eight hundred thousand pieces. Copied from drawings, engravings, bookplates and even seals, these services sailed back at the rate of one every six days for a century, averaging about five for every direct sailing from Canton. As the century progressed, the arms, which at first fitted into the Chinese design, began to dominate the heavily decorated porcelain, then were painted more modestly on the centre or rim with European scrolls (copied from Meissen and later from English factories); and finally, as duties on Chinese porcelain reached the prohibitive level of 150 per cent to protect the growing factories in England, the decoration became thin and mechanical and the arms were neatly tucked into ermine mantling. It is small wonder that even the East India Company ordered their armorial service from Spode in 1820.

Most of the great houses which are now in the care of the National Trust must have had armorial services although, as these ceased to be made a century and a half ago, many had left their original homes before the Trust could know them. Such a case is Hanbury, where a single piece of the two fine services made about 1725 for the Vernon family is all that remains in the house. At Stourhead, the home of the Hoare family for two centuries, there are a number of pieces of two fine Yung Chêng tea-services made about 1730 with their arms (pl. 141). These were the earliest, and most striking, of four services made for the family. There are fine services at Shugborough (c. 1743) (pl. 139), Uppark (c. 1760), Arlington (c. 1765), Ickworth (c. 1780), and Nostell (c. 1790) (pl. 151), while at Trerice in Cornwall the small collection of armorial porcelain includes a dish of the rare Ker-Martin service (c. 1795) with panels representing the four known continents.

The display of two hundred and five dishes and plates of the Anson service at Shugborough is as impressive as the design is important in the history of ceramics (pl. 139). Each circular dish and plate (like so many other services of the first half of the eighteenth century, this includes no other pieces) has an anchor painted on the reverse. The obverse carries views of Plymouth Sound, Whampoa (the anchorage twelve miles downstream from Canton), and a mythical scene derived almost certainly from Captain Piercy Brett's notebook. He was Commodore (later Admiral) Anson's artist on the *Centurion*, and after three gruelling months on Tenian Island, collecting breadfruit trees for the colonies of the West Indies, it was appropriate that he should incorporate this tree in his design. In a mahogany display cabinet at Shugborough in 'Chinese Chippendale' style, flanked by fine Chinese mirror paintings, are part of two other *famille verte* dinner-services used by the Admiral, though of an earlier date.

The two armorial services of the Fetherstonhaugh family at Uppark are unusual; both incorporate designs unique to armorial porcelain, probably copied from Worcester although Chelsea examples exist. When Sir Matthew bought the property in 1747 it would have been difficult to predict that his daughter-in-law's sister would still be living there in 1895, but such was the case. He had married Sarah Lethieullier of a Huguenot banking family in 1746, and the Lethieulliers already had a number of armorial services. His son was to befriend the sixteen-year-old Emma Hart, who was later to enthral Nelson, and she is said to have danced on his dinner-table before his guests (and his porcelain). She must have gazed too at the wonderful dolls' house complete with its Chinese porcelain tea-service, of about 1750, in miniature scale with cups barely an inch across (pl. 134).

It is a popular belief that the Chinese miscopied European arms, and their so-called errors are often pointed out with mild amusement. But it can hardly have been the Chinese who, on the Chichesters' tea- and dinner-service at Arlington, invented cinquefoils when roundels were required in the Courtenay quartering, nor they who chose one quarter only of the MacDonald arms (and that incorrectly) for Miss MacDonald who married Colonel John Chichester of Arlington as his second wife in 1764. Such errors did not occur in the great and meticulous service now at Ickworth, probably made in 1780 for Captain John Augustus Hervey who married Elizabeth Drummond of Quebec in 1779 and in the same year became Lord Hervey. The most charming pieces of this service are a pair of chestnut bowls.

Of all services of porcelain with British armorials the rich, heavily gilt service at Nostell(pl. 151) is the largest one known. It is strewn with a variety of small panels enclosing scenes and sprays of flowers in sepia, and was made perhaps for Alexander Hannay, Adjutant General in India and Commander of the Army of the King of Oude, or for his brother Ramsay, a merchant trading between India and China. The exact date that it came to Nostell is not known, but both brothers were dead before 1820 and about that time the Winn family were making great acquisitions. Perhaps only from the nineteenth century onwards would it have been possible to buy such a service without feeling embarrassed by arms which were other than one's own. Here is an early example of that desire to collect 'antique' porcelain which was to blossom later in the century and to grow out of all recognition in the twentieth.

As late as the second half of the eighteenth century a 'collection' of porcelain was rare, and one can witness in the two branches of the Parker family—at Saltram and Long Melford—the more usual pattern of acquisition for use. John Parker of Saltram House, M.P. for Devon from 1762, and created Lord Boringdon in 1784, was a man of taste who employed Chippendale and Robert Adam, and sat to Reynolds. Perhaps a number of pairs of blue vases, with gilding in the style of 1760 and formal dragon handles, were gifts from his cousin Captain Parker who stayed at Saltram on a number of occasions after sailing into Plymouth. The very unusual monk's cap ewer and basin in *famille rose* (pl. 138) may even have come from the great prize which Captain Parker captured in 1762. The Parkers also acquired at least three Chinese dinner-services: the first about 1760, in pseudo tobacco-leaf pattern; a second about

1775; and finally in 1810 an imposing late dessert-service of European shapes with wine-coolers and centrepiece, today still in the dining-room and possibly replacing an earlier underglaze blue service made in Japan with hexagonal moulded and gadrooned rims, *c.* 1750, of which a few plates remain in the kitchen.

Long Melford has a collection of porcelain of even more interest to the connoisseur. There are a number of fine early Chinese and Japanese dishes in *famille verte* and Imari, the most important being a huge Japanese Imari circular charger with a central coat-of-arms painted about 1710 almost certainly for the Dutch market. But of greater importance is the porcelain acquired by Captain Hyde Parker in October 1762, when he captured the *Santissima Trinidad*. A share of the prize fell to him including a cargo of porcelain said to have been intended for the Spanish court.

There are at least six pairs of covered vases including two of gigantic size now on the main stairway, which certainly came from this prize. A number of circular dishes are of the same distinctive orange, sepia and gold design (with pheasants and phoenix) which was much to the Spaniards' liking (pl. 145). Some delightful tea and chocolate services in very fine porcelain with lotus-petal and *bianco-sopra-bianco* decoration were probably in the same prize and a careful analysis may yield more claimants. It is an interesting feature that much of this ware would normally be thought to be a little earlier—from 1745-55—and this may be partly because it was a special cargo of the very best quality and partly because supplies from China had been much delayed after 1756, on account of the Seven Years War. Not from this cargo, but also of interest, are the considerable remains of a Parker armorial service of about 1765, and two pairs of large Chinese saucer-dishes of a Japanese style in underglaze blue with unusual moulded rims, which are identical in all other respects (but that they have no Walpole armorials under the base) to a service made for Horatio, Baron Walpole in either 1752 or 1756.

Of course, it was easier to inherit porcelain by marriage than to capture it on the high seas and this was the lot of Sir John Trevelyan of Wallington who married in 1771 Maria Wilson 'whose marriage portion was a magnificent collection of china, the greater part of it Chinese'. She herself was deeply interested in her own dowry and still watches over part of it from her portrait by Hoppner at Wallington. But not all the earlier porcelain at Wallington had come with Maria Wilson, for in 1769 a visitor wrote of the Saloon (which today has two recessed oval cabinets set in plasterwork and filled with early eighteenth-century porcelain pieces): 'In one corner of the room is a noble china cistern.' This was the massive Chinese fish bowl of *c.* 1750 which stands on a rare wooden stand with dolphin feet (pl 147), and is visible in the portrait of Sir Walter Trevelyan by William Bell Scott.

Another collection of porcelain was to come to Wallington with Sir Charles

133 Detail of a Chinese mirror-painting; the figure is reputedly the Emperor Ch'ien Lung at his Summer Palace in Peking   Shugborough

134 Part of a Chinese doll's-house tea-set, Ch'ien Lung period, *c*. 1750   Cups 1 in. wide Uppark

135 Burghley House teapot:
16th-century Chinese jar
and cover with later silver
mounts   Ht 8¾ in., w. 8½ in.
Anglesey Abbey

136 Ming dish, Tšuan Tê
period, 1426–35
Diam. 17 in.   Wallington

137 A corner of Mrs Lucy's ▶
boudoir: 19th-century
Chinese washbasin,
jug and plates
Charlecote Park

138 Chinese basin, ewer and cover in the form of a 'monk's cap', Ch'ien Lung period, *c.* 1750
Ewer: ht 11¼ in., w. 9 in.; basin: w. 10 in.   Saltram House

139 Plate from the 'Breadfruit' armorial service, Canton, 1743   Diam. 9 in.   Shugborough

140 Japanese Arita bottle, the body enamelled in Holland, late 17th century   Ht 17 in.
    Buscot Park

141 Part of a Chinese tea-service, Yung Chêng period, *c.* 1730   Stourhead

143 Japanese Kakiemon fish, mounted as a *fontaine à parfum*, 18th century   Ht 14 in. ▶
Waddesdon Manor

142 Famille verte horses and riders, early Ching Dynasty, 1645–60   Ht (l.) 6⅝ in., (r.) 8 in.
Ascott

144 Japanese Kutani bowl, late 17th century, with French silver mounts   Ht 8 in., diam. 8½ in.
Sizergh Castle

145 Pair of Chinese vases and a plate (one of a pair), Ch'ien Lung period, 1745–55
Vases: ht 22 in.; plate: w. 22 in.   Melford Hall

146 Japanese Arita eagles, *c.* 1710   Ht 22 in.   Waddesdon Manor

148 Suite of silver furniture: table, looking-glass and tripod stands, London marks, 1676 and 1680   Knole

◀ 147 Famille rose fish bowl, Ch'ien Lung period, *c.* 1750   Bowl: ht 15 in., diam. 24 in. Wallington

149 Chinese octagonal dish, K'ang Hsi period, *c.* 1710   W. 7⅛ in.   Fenton House

150 One of a pair of Chinese goose tureens, Ch'ien Lung period, *c.* 1760   Ht 13½ in.
     Polesden Lacey

151 Tureen from the Hannay Chinese armorial service, Ch'ien Lung period, *c.* 1790
     Ht 12 in., w. 15 in.   Nostell Priory

152 Silver-gilt cake-basket (one of a pair), by Paul de Lamerie, London mark, 1731
   L. 12 in.   Ickworth

154 Race-cup and cover by Smith and Sharp from Adam's design, London mark, 1764 ▶
   Ht 19 in., w. 16 in.   Anglesey Abbey

153 Wine cistern by Robert Cooper, London mark, 1680   L. 27 in.   Ickworth

155 View of the Hunting Room, with some of Mrs Gubbay's collection of Chinese Ch'ien Lung
period birds, 1736–95   Clandon Park

Trevelyan, who had been a distinguished Indian civil servant and Governor of Madras, his acquisitions being marked 'Lucknow 1859'. The whole was rearranged two years after Sir Charles's death in 1886 by his son, Sir George Otto Trevelyan, who wrote in his notebook, 'This year I finished rearranging the china, a long and delightful labour of love ...'

His work is still intact and there are numerous cabinets of blue-and-white, Chinese and Japanese Imari, *famille verte* and a lesser number of export *famille rose*. Exceptional, even here, is the early fifteenth-century blue-and-white Ming dish painted with lotus flowers and with an incised Arabic inscription on the base, 'Year one of King Shah Jahan, Warrior of the Faith', betraying its presence in that Mogul Emperor's treasury in 1628 (pl. 136). A large *famille verte* dish has the arms of Gelderland, while a barber's bowl has the arms of Vlaanderen: these are examples from two of the three series of such dishes made for the Dutch market between 1700 and 1720.

Collecting presupposes buying, but unlike pictures porcelain is difficult to trace through the salerooms unless it is a piece of outstanding merit. At Charlecote the only pieces which can be so traced came from Fonthill in 1822. There is no evidence that the Lucy family, who had lived at Charlecote since the twelfth century, had bought porcelain in the eighteenth, for they were prosperous country gentlemen in a central part of England isolated from mercantile adventure, where their rich Warwickshire land was far more important than foreign trade. However, the Reverend John Lucy went to Fonthill the year before he died and bought the great four-poster bed of carved ebony from Ceylon and 'quantities of porcelain.' It is difficult to say with certainty what comes from William Beckford's fabulous home, apart from a pair of ruby ground vases in the Great Hall and a number of pieces with ormolu mounts, but a finely enamelled small bowl in translucent blue, green and russet, with gilt decoration, would also have been exactly to Mr Beckford's taste. Though not always open to the public, Mrs Lucy's boudoir at Charlecote, which has remained unaltered since she died in 1886, is of particular interest. It contains a late nineteenth-century washstand, made by a Warwickshire carpenter, with contemporary Chinese ewer and bowl, while the walls are decked with indifferent Chinese and European plates on Victorian circular velvet mounts, hung sometimes singly between photographs and sometimes in vertical strings of threes and fours. Here we may see how modest Chinese porcelain was used and displayed a century ago (pl. 137). In most country houses all such evidence has long since been swept away.

Although there are smaller selections of porcelain at Lanhydrock near Bodmin, at Knole and at Petworth, six important collections of Chinese porcelain in the care of the Trust and made within living memory lie in easy reach of London: at Ascott, Waddesdon, Buscot, Fenton, Polesden Lacey and Clandon. It would be idle to imagine that any brief description could do

M

justice to collections of such breadth and variety. They are unlike the other porcelain in Trust houses (except perhaps Wallington) in that all pieces were collected for their beauty and rarity in an age which had ceased to regard Chinese porcelain as an expendable, every-day commodity. They illustrate the expertise of the collector of the last hundred years, his greater knowledge, his specialization and his balanced taste.

Two collections formed by members of the Rothschild family are only a few miles apart in Buckinghamshire. That at Ascott, where a member of the family still lives, is the only porcelain collection in the care of the Trust which stretches back to the seventh century, to a time when the early Saxon kings were conquering Britain and the T'ang Dynasty ruled in China. In fact in this entire collection there are possibly only two pieces which show a trace of the *famille rose* enamel introduced in 1721–2. The collection spans a thousand years and selects a few periods of special interest which well illustrate the whole: figures and vessels of the T'ang Dynasty; beautiful bowls and dishes of the Sung Dynasty (960–1279) in fathomless delicate blues; the Ming Dynasty (1368–1644) represented by specialized selections of vessels and figures of stoneware and porcelain, some in *san ts'ai* (three-colour) decoration, particularly turquoise, deep violet, aubergine and yellow (but no wares of underglaze blue); and the early Ching Dynasty—*famille verte* with an exciting collection of figures, horses held and ridden (pl. 142)—which illustrate in their effective formal simplicity the hand of the Chinese potter before the Western merchants demanded more naturalistic animals. The collection of Mr Anthony de Rothschild and his father, Mr Leopold de Rothschild of Gunnersbury Park, are today beautifully and sympathetically displayed at Ascott.

At Waddesdon Mr James de Rothschild, his father Baron Edward and *his* cousin Baron Ferdinand (who built the house between 1874 and 1889 and died in 1898) are together responsible for the oriental porcelain which forms only a small part of the collection. The Chinese porcelain is predominantly to French taste: graceful bowls and vases in deep blue and purple, lavender and turquoise, mounted in the richest ormolu of the eighteenth and nineteenth centuries, and some datable before 1749. More startling are a pair of early eighteenth-century Japanese eagles (pl. 146) standing twenty-two inches tall and predating similar eagles made at the Meissen factory about 1733. Nor can there be a finer upright fish than that decorated in the most vivid Kakiemon style and encrusted with ormolu as a *fontaine-à-parfum* (pl. 143).

The Faringdon collection at Buscot Park contains some exceptional pieces: blue-and-white after 1680, fine *famille verte* and Imari vases, and in the saloon one of the rare personalized pieces to have survived from the seventeenth century—a heavy bottle of Japanese Arita ware (with later Dutch decoration) and on the base the initials I C (pl. 140). These are possibly for Johannes Camphuys, between 1671 and 1675 the principal Dutch merchant on the Japanese island of Deshima, in the Bay of Nagasaki, which was the headquarters of the Dutch trading in Japan. (Another blue-and-white vase of this date is known with these initials.) There are also three fine chargers with arms of about 1735 in the dining-room.

By contrast Fenton is demure and precise. Lady Binning found space, among her exceptional collection of European porcelain, for three rooms of oriental ware. The collection of K'ang Hsi blue-and-white in the Blue Porcelain Room is an echo of the Victoria and Albert Museum where the greater part of the Salting Collection is now displayed, and the Oriental Room has a small selection of *blanc de chine*. Some of the porcelain has excellent lineage, for in the book case is a catalogue prepared in 1914 entitled 'Mrs M. E. Salting ... A Descriptive Inventory of Porcelains ... at 49 Berkeley Square, edited by George Stoner, King Street, St. James's.' Many of the pieces at Fenton can be identified from this inventory. One other modest piece requires mention: a small octagonal *famille verte* dish of Chinese porcelain in Japanese taste which bears the incised 'Johanneum mark' of the first great European collector of oriental porcelain, Augustus the Strong, Elector of Saxony (pl. 149).

Mrs Greville left at Polesden Lacey massive vases and smaller garnitures displayed in the corridors on three sides of a central courtyard; a quiet library with shelves topped by Chinese blue-and-white and Japanese Imari, dating from the late seventeenth century to the early eighteenth; and in the hall a pair of magnificent soup tureens in the form of geese which were made in considerable quantities about 1750 for the European market (pl. 150). But it is the glittering drawing-room, panelled and mirrored, with its sumptuous French furniture, that displays her collection of *famille verte* and *famille rose* dishes and vases, figures and birds. It is a mark of the fineness of this porcelain that even in such opulent surroundings each piece demands attention on its own account.

At Clandon three eighteenth-century rooms provide a stately home for Mrs Gubbay's peerless collection of oriental birds and animals. Only the eagles at Waddesdon are missing! But without them this must still be the greatest porcelain aviary in existence. The watchful hawks and supercilious cranes stand on remarkable giltwood brackets, with resplendent peacocks, aggressive cocks and the occasional aloof goose; three *famille verte* hounds support a bowl, an alert hare crouches immovable, while ducks sail serenely past as if they had always lived on polished cabinets. The *famille verte* birds (pl. 155) seem ruffled by the greater splendour of their *famille rose* companions. Yet all are frozen on their perches. If you watch for movement, the preening of feathers, or listen for a sound, there is none. They are only Chinese porcelain.

9

English Silver

Robert Rowe

Silver chattels have certain unique characteristics which it might be wise to dwell upon briefly before thinking about the silver content of National Trust houses. The most fundamental of these qualities proceeds from the fact that the material is bullion and therefore every silver—or gold—object has, and as far as we can see always will have, a value quite distinct from its form and function. Since the metal is precious and re-usable, silver chattels have been at special risk from their owners' economic circumstances as well as from the importance they attached to changes in fashion. During much of its existence therefore, the plate in National Trust houses has had the spectre of the melting-pot hovering over it. That this spectre has faded in the twentieth century is due to a change in the climate of opinion: today we revere the arts of the past with the result that the 'antique' value of an object is usually much greater than that of its bullion content. For the same reason a piece of silver is unlikely to be 'improved' now, a practice our forebears saw nothing against.

Through the ages silver has frequently been the material of masterpieces and quite a number of these are in National Trust hands. Fine specimens have been discovered in plate rooms, usually dark and mysterious places which can present inventory makers with conditions not unlike those of an archaeological dig, occasionally offering startling rewards, but more predictably lungs full of dust. At the other end of the spectrum come the well documented collections formed as such. Those at Polesden Lacey and Anglesey Abbey are good examples of a comparatively modern phenomenon as, before the middle of the last century (apart from trophies), no one but an eccentric would have thought seriously of collecting, as opposed to using, silver. Between these two extremes come the magnificent family possessions now in the Trust's care, those at Knole and Ickworth for instance, which are so much part of the history and presence of those houses that to alienate them would be unthinkable.

On the whole, plate was more independent of the fabric of the house in which it resided than its friends and relations, among them furniture and ceramics. The most movable of movables, it was often made specifically for bringing out on special occasions and putting away again, partly because it became tarnished and therefore needed frequent cleaning, but also no doubt because it was relatively light and physically tough—an accident was rarely fatal. The nearest silver came to being tied to the house was when it could be confused with furniture. Hybrid though it may be, silver furniture was a splendid advertisement for its owner.

Hybrids aside, silver plate as a species is one of the most difficult things to show to advantage in a country house. There are daunting security risks and provision has seldom been made for its permanent display. Pictures, sculpture and antiquities on the other hand—those traditional playthings, or mental exercisers, what you will, of the rich—sometimes had galleries specially built for them which, together with their contents, became an important element in the character of a building. Furniture was frequently acquired to embellish state rooms or was designed to be an essential part of a suite of rooms so that to separate one from the other would be to spoil the whole. The nomadic role assigned to silver has meant that its historical resting place is the plate room. It seems inevitable, therefore, that the silver is often the least known of the treasures which should be enjoyed in a house open to the public. It is a pity, if acceptable at all, that such riches should be seen mainly in temporary exhibitions out of context and often miles from home. Showcases are unhistorical certainly, but then the way of life for which a mansion house was built is little more than a memory in 1976. Works of art may be timeless wonders, but they can be made to look better—or worse—by their immediate surroundings. It is often said that a museum atmosphere must be avoided, but all great houses were designed to have a museum function in the true sense: to display, to all those considered eligible for such delights, the objects acquired by the wealth, taste and knowledge of the owner. The business of providing a home for the family, only during part of the year in any case, did not conflict with this idea.

The purpose of this article is to introduce, or remind visitors of, the plate belonging to the houses they may plan to see. A chronological survey, even if it were desirable, would not be possible for if all the National Trust silver were put together it would present a picture of richness in one period and poverty in another. This makes it all the more interesting. To suggest a time span, however, individual pieces and occasionally collections, especially if they present a coherent whole, will be taken in approximate date order—with occasional divergences—beginning with the oldest and ending with the youngest.

The obvious starting point is the font-shaped gilt cup (pl. 156) discovered at Charlecote just after the Second World War. Tudor secular plate is exceedingly rare, even so this cup, bearing the London mark for 1524, belongs to a fairly well defined family group with many characteristics in common. Some had covers, others did not. Aesthetically the Charlecote cup is a strange device, but its very oddity and boldness give it a presence. Better described perhaps as a 'happening' than a design, it stands somewhere between the Gothic and Renaissance styles and its various parts seem to be arrogantly unrelated to each other. From the comparatively delicate engraved cartouches round the bowl which contain some personable beasts taken from fact and fable—a hedgehog, a coursing hound and a monkey are easily recognizable—the eye descends past a 'feathered' stem to a foot of massive gadroons. The effect is as incongruous as a hobnailed boot at a ball. Nevertheless this cup does introduce some of the most admirable qualities of all subsequent English silver. Our craftsmen have always relished the material they worked with, the possibilities of which they sometimes exploited with careless abandon. Never over-impressed by art history, motifs of wide diversity of type and origin were often combined and misunderstood with great success. One suspects that this fresh approach is not so naive as it first appears and maybe it has something to do with the very positive British genius for compromise; an attribute, incidentally, which could bring death to the arts of other countries.

Nearly a century and a half later the restoration of the monarchy produced another period of unabashed vigour superbly represented by the silver at Knole. The suite of furniture dating from around 1680 complete with its looking-glass, table and pair of candlestands, must be one of the most magnificent ever conceived or made (pl. 148). It sums up the swift-passing baroque in England where this style, so significant on the Continent, was seen mainly as an excuse for extravagance and the release of energy. Never once, it seems, did the maker, whose ability as a silversmith matched his inspiration, question the validity of what he was doing. There is something inherently bogus about silver furniture: it was always impractical, for the thin silver sheets used covered wooden and iron frames, making it both heavy and fragile and almost impossible to keep clean. There were no silver lacquers in the seventeenth century. Yet most of the silver furniture still extant—that in the royal collections and the very fine group, which includes chairs, in Rosenborg Castle, Copenhagen (also an erstwhile royal collection)—has the capacity to lift the heart. It is a slightly uncomfortable thought that so much of the art of the past which gives us the most pleasure was produced for socially deplorable reasons, by mid-twentieth-century standards; in the case of silver furniture for the display of wealth and power by kings and courtiers. The silver bed made for Nell Gwyn in 1674 may well provoke a shudder of self-righteousness. Its precious metal weighed 2,265 oz., as we know from the bill which survives as evidence of a lavish age.

In a great house like Knole or on a smaller scale Ham, equally splendid in its furnishings, silver garniture for the chimney-pieces was considered essential. At Knole there are still five pairs of silver fire dogs, among the most attractive being those of about 1670 surmounted by 'winking cupids' (pl. 157). At Ham there is a fine pair of bellows of the same period, one side of which is almost entirely covered in silver filigree work (pl. 159). Silver sconces in the late seventeenth century and early eighteenth century played no less important a part in the internal countenance of such houses. The most practical of all the symbols of success displayed by their owners, the polished back-plates reflected the light of the candle. They were however very vulnerable; of thin metal they suffered from the ministrations of ham-fisted servants who continually had to replace the candles. Added to this hazard they went out of fashion before the middle of the eighteenth century and many were consequently melted down. Nevertheless, twenty-six survive at Knole, including the armorial set of twelve, dated 1685 (pl. 158), among the finest of their kind left and displaying the richness of which this art form was capable. There is a fine pair at Erddig too of about the same time. Also to be found at Knole is the pretty toilet set of 1673 (pl. 160); an early manifestation of this luxurious fashion, the oval hairbrushes suggest that it may have been adapted for male use. It seems certain that all such sets were originally made for the fair sex.

When grandeur was the key to fashion whimsy provided a welcome escape and some of the best silversmiths of the day were party to it. The group of chinoiserie silver at Polesden Lacey, much of it assiduously collected around 1900, illustrates this well. The flat-chased designs may suggest the current occidental view of Cathay and 'chinamen', but they are really conscious bits of oriental nonsense. Usually embellishing the simplest objects this surface decoration, in vogue only from about 1675 to 1690, is seen at its most charming in the pair of small mugs—incidentally very rare—made by the well-known silversmith George Garthorne in 1685 (pl. 161). Over a century later 'Regency' silver, whatever its merits, was heavy and ponderous and, sure enough, it produced its whimsical antidote, again usually concocted by the leading makers. At Knole for example is a pair of gilt candlesticks decorated with swans, shells and foliage, and at Buscot an inkstand in the form of a water lily. All bear the mark of John Bridge and are highly sophisticated creations. By the second half of our own century most commissioned plate was made for, or on behalf of, civic corporations and other public bodies; inevitably some of the pomposity of such patrons was reflected in the objects made for them. The occasional domestic piece—there are a few in the Anglesey Abbey collection—frequently has an even stronger whimsical element than its seventeenth-century counterpart.

The arrival in England of those Huguenot refugees who were, or became, silversmiths, had far-reaching results. Their work was immediately admired, to the chagrin of native craftsmen, for it appeared to be quite new at a time when patrons were tiring of flimsy silver decorated within a limited repertoire of ornament. The much-held view that the best English silver was produced during the Huguenot heyday, between about 1690 and 1730, is not quite so confused as it may seem: the foreigners were making their contribution to the craft in the country of their adoption; the English, though jealous, were soon aware that the strangers were on to something and a mutual absorption took place with the result that in the ancestry of most subsequent good design provincial Frenchmen stand beside metropolitan Englishmen. Many of the refugees were minor gentry in their own country and would have lost caste by engaging in trade. Silversmithing was different, however, for it involved bullion and so could be considered banking. That the Huguenots were familiar with the high fashion, as well as its decorative sources, prevailing in the court circles of Louis XIV and indeed that their own possessions, in some measure at least, reflected it, may reasonably be assumed. They came to England often with little more than knowledge, taste and determination, though some were already highly skilled. The Huguenot style, particularly in the hands of the younger generation who grew up here, with its cast mouldings, strap-work and cut-card detail contrasting with plain surfaces, chasing and engraving —all helping to emphasize carefully considered shapes and proportions— contains all the best elements of the French manner perfectly adapted to a new market. There is certainly invention too, which was no doubt mothered by necessity.

Some superb Huguenot silver belongs to the National Trust. A ewer at Attingham, made almost certainly for purely decorative purposes by David Willaume in 1715 (pl. 162), and an earlier tankard by the same maker at Polesden Lacey (pl. 163), sum up the skills of the first generation of immigrant craftsmen. The fame of Willaume is matched by that of Philip Rollos whose work may be seen at its most magnificent in a pair of wine-coolers at Ickworth (pl. 164).

There can be no better introduction to the plate at Ickworth which gives such a clear picture of a rich nobleman's possessions in the middle of the eighteenth century. The earliest piece is the wine-cistern made by the Englishman Robert Cooper in 1680 (pl. 153). Not so big as the one he made the following year for the Earl of Rutland, or so spectacular as those made by Willaume and Rollos for other noble patrons, it is nevertheless quite able to stand on its own feet—in the form of four sturdy dolphins. Paul de Lamerie is well represented here. The most famous of the silversmiths of Huguenot extraction he also has a good claim to be placed among the greatest designer-craftsmen reared in this country; a fine example of his skill is a cake-basket of 1731 (pl. 152). Although he was brought here before his first birthday his work often presents an unmistakably French personality, well seen in the shallow dessert-dish of 1724 (pl. 165). Perhaps the most remarkable feature of the Ickworth plate is the number—some twenty-two pieces or sets—and the quality of the contribution by Frederick Kandler, who later became a leading neo-classical silversmith. A much admired representative of a gifted family of German origin he was commissioned in the 1750s and 60s to make pairs and sets from Lamerie pieces, including the dish and cake-basket illustrated. This

156 Gilt font-shaped cup, 1524, maker's mark a mullet   Ht 4¾ in.   Charlecote Park

157 Andiron (one of a pair), *c.* 1670   Ht 24 in.
Knole

158 Sconce (one of twelve), *c.* 1685, maker's
mark TS, crowns above
Ht 9¾ in., w. 7 in.   Knole

159 Silver-mounted bellows, *c.* 1675   L. 20¼ in., w. 7 in.   Ham House

160 Parcel-gilt toilet set, London mark, *c.* 1673   Knole

161 Pair of mugs by George Garthorne, London mark, 1685   Ht 3 in.   Polesden Lacey

162 Ewer by David Willaume,
London mark, 1715   Ht 11½ in., w. 10½ in.
Attingham Park

163 Tankard by David Willaume,
London mark, 1701
Ht 8 in.   Polesden Lacey

164 Pair of wine-coolers by Philip Rollos, London mark, *c.* 1715 Ht 10½ in. Ickworth

165 Silver-gilt dessert dish by Paul de Lamerie, London mark, 1724 L. 13¼ in. Ickworth

166 Wine cooler (from a set of twelve) by Paul Storr, London mark, 1812
Ht 11¼ in., w. 10½ in.   Petworth House

167 Three-light candelabrum
(from a set of twelve)
by Simon le Sage,
London mark, 1758
Ht 18 in., w. 14½ in.
Ickworth

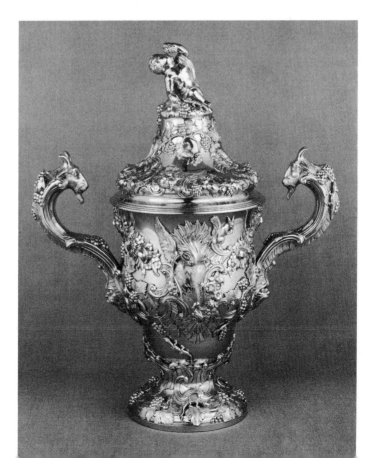

168 Cup and cover by
Peter Taylor,
London mark, 1746
Ht 17 in., w. 14½ in.
Anglesey Abbey

169 Soup tureen (one of a pair) by Frederick Kandler, London mark, 1752   L. 13¾ in.
     Ickworth
170 Vegetable dish by Paul Storr, London mark, 1829   Ht 9 in., l. 13½ in.   Anglesey Abbey

difficult exercise proved his craftsmanship to be the equal of his models while his original work, epitomized by the pair of soup tureens of 1752 in the full rococo manner (pl. 169), showed him to have been a designer of no mean powers. In this house also is a superb set of twelve three-light candelabra of 1758 by Simon le Sage (pl. 167). These employ almost every conceivable rococo twist and turn, including caryatid figures, and yet everything fits together very happily.

There is a fine collection of cups at Anglesey Abbey acquired with great discernment. One of them, made in 1746 (pl. 168), by Peter Taylor well demonstrates that quality of uninhibited imagination so encouraged by the rococo. It makes an excellent and instructive contrast with another cup in the same collection, made in 1764 by Daniel Smith and Robert Sharp to a design, now in the Soane Museum, by Robert Adam (pl. 154). In architecture and the decorative arts the work of Adam represents the first phase of the neo-classical movement. Shapes and decoration were based on those of classical antiquity, but freely interpreted to create a new and easily recognizable style. The Anglesey cup was certainly an 'invention' in the sense in which this word was used at the time. The same makers were commissioned to produce an almost identical cup as the prize for the Richmond races of 1764 and continued to make variants, for these races, at least until 1770. It is well to remember, particularly at this period, that the demand for trophies provided opportunities for silversmiths to produce masterpieces displaying all their skills and knowledge; they were working for critical customers who knew a good deal about the classical sources from which they sprang and also admired Robert Adam, who had taken polite society by storm.

The last phase of the neo-classical period may be discerned in what is generally called Regency silver. The mixture now had considerable archaeological content filtered through the minds of sculptors, architects and painters and leavened by the often inspired silver of eighteenth-century France. Without the designs of William Theed, John Flaxman, Charles Heathcote Tatham and Thomas Stothard, all of whom thought in terms of marble and stone rather than of gold and silver—plus the plate of, for example, Thomas Germain and Henry Auguste, sold in London by families fleeing from the French Revolution—the products of the famous firm Rundell Bridge and Rundell and the superb craftsmanship associated with the names of Paul Storr, the two Smiths and Digby Scott, would have been unthinkable. If you add to all this the fact that the renewal of war with France in 1803 led to rent increases profiting the landed gentry who were thus able to emulate royal extravagance, it is not surprising that Rundell died a millionaire or that many of the larger National Trust houses contain fine early nineteenth-century plate. The wine-cooler of 1812 from a set of twelve by Storr at Petworth (pl. 166), is typical and has features in common with others he made, while a set of four vegetable-dishes, of 1829 at

Anglesey, all surmounted by different vegetable finials, show his strength on a more domestic level (pl. 170).

To round off this brief sketch it would be fair to say that from the National Trust collections one can learn little of the creative controversies which made up the history of English silver after the Great Exhibition of 1851, and by 1860 the visual feast is over.

Books for further reading

PAINTING

Anthony Blunt, *Art and Architecture in France 1500–1700. Pelican History of Art*, 1970.

S. J. Freedberg, *Painting in Italy 1500–1600. Pelican History of Art*, 1970.

J. M. Friedländer, *From Van Eyck to Brueghel*, 1969.

H. Gerson and E. H. ter Kuile, *Art and Architecture in Belgium 1600–1800, Pelican History of Art*, 1960.

Cecil Gould, *Introduction to Renaissance Painting in Italy*, 1957.

George Kubler and M. Soria, *Art and Architecture in Spain and Portugal and their American Dominions. Pelican History of Art*, 1959.

Michael Levey and W. G. Kalnein, *Art and Architecture of the Eighteenth Century in France. Pelican History of Art*, 1972.

The Oxford History of English Art, 4 vols., 1952–7.

J. Rosenberg, S. Slive and E. H. ter Kuile, *Dutch Art and Architecture 1600–1800. Pelican History of Art*, 1966.

W. Stechow, *Dutch Landscape Painting of the Seventeenth Century*, 1966.

Ellis Waterhouse, *Painting in Britain 1530–1790. Penguin History of Art*, 1953.

SCULPTURE

Rupert Gunnis, *Dictionary of British Sculptors 1660–1851*, 1953.

A. T. F. Michaelis, *Ancient Marbles in Great Britain*, Cambridge, 1882.

Margaret I. Webb, *Michael Rysbrack, Sculptor*, 1954.

Margaret Whinney, *Sculpture in Britain 1530–1830. Pelican History of Art*, 1964.

TAPESTRY AND NEEDLEWORK

A. F. Kendrick, *English Needlework*, 1967.

H. C. Marillier, *English Tapestries of the Eighteenth Century*, 1930.

W. G. Thomson, *Tapestry Weaving in England*, 1914.

—— *A History of Tapestry*, 1973.

G. Wingfield Digby, *Elizabethan Embroidery*, 1963.

ENGLISH FURNITURE

Elizabeth Aslin, *Nineteenth-Century English Furniture*, 1962.

Ralph Edwards, *Shorter Dictionary of English Furniture*, 1964.

R. Edwards and M. Jourdain, *Georgian Cabinet Makers*, 1954.
Ralph Fastnedge, *English Furniture Styles 1500–1830*, 1955.
Hugh Honour, *Cabinet Makers and Furniture Designers*, 1969.
Maurice Tomlin, *English Furniture*, 1972.

FRENCH FURNITURE

Geoffrey de Bellaigue, *The James A. de Rothschild Collection at Waddesdon Manor: Furniture, Clocks and Gilt Bronzes*, 2 vols., Fribourg, 1975.
Comte François de Salverte, *Les Ébénistes du XVIIIe Siècle*, Paris, 1934.
G. Souchal, *Le Mobilier Français au XVIIIe Siècle*, 1961.
Pierre Verlet, *Le Style Louis XV*, Paris, 1942.
—— *Le Mobilier Royal Français*, 2 vols., Paris, 1945–55.
—— *L'Art du Meuble à Paris au XVIIIe Siècle*, Paris, 1958.
F. J. B. Watson, *Furniture. Wallace Collection Catalogue*, 1956.
—— *Louis XVI Furniture*, 1960.
R. A. Weigert, *Le Style Louis XVI*, Paris, 1941.

EUROPEAN POTTERY AND PORCELAIN

R. J. Charleston (ed.), *World Ceramics*, 1968.
F. H. Garner and M. Archer, *English Delftware*, 1972.
W. B. Honey, *French Porcelain of the Eighteenth Century*, 1972.
C. H. de Jonge, *Delft Ceramics*, 1970.
G. Lewis, *A Collector's History of English Pottery*, 1969.
G. Wills, *English Pottery and Porcelain*, 1969.

PORCELAIN FROM CHINA AND JAPAN

John Ayers, *The James A. de Rothschild Collection at Waddesdon Manor: Oriental Porcelain*, Fribourg, 1971.
Michel Beurdeley, *Porcelain of the East India Companies*, 1962.
Anthony du Boulay, *Chinese Porcelain*, 1963.
David S. Howard, *Chinese Armorial Porcelain*, 1974.
Soame Jenyns, *Later Chinese Porcelain: the Ching Dynasty (1644–1912)*, 1951.
Margaret Jourdain and Soame Jenyns, *Chinese Export Art in the Eighteenth Century*, 1950.
John G. Phillips, *China Trade Porcelain*, Cambridge, Mass., 1956.
D. F. Lunsingh Scheurleer, *Chinese Export Porcelain: Chine de Commande*, 1974.

SILVER

Michael Clayton, *Collector's Dictionary of the Silver and Gold of Great Britain and North America*, 1971.
A. Grimwade, *Rococo Silver 1727–1765*, 1974.
J. F. Hayward, *Huguenot Silver in England 1688–1727*, 1959.
Charles Oman, *English Domestic Silver*, 1968.
—— *Caroline Silver 1625–1688*, 1975.
Robert Rowe, *Adam Silver 1765–1795*, 1965.
Gerald Taylor, *Silver Through the Ages*, 1956.

Principal Collections in National Trust Houses

The inclusion of a house in this list does not necessarily mean that the contents belong to the Trust. Certain collections are the property of the Government (e.g. at Ham and Osterley), others are in private ownership (e.g. at Nostell Priory), and yet others belong partly to the Trust and partly to private owners. Houses are not listed whose contents are primarily of interest, not as works of art, but for their association with famous people (e.g. Bateman's, Carlyle's House, Chartwell, Smallhythe).

Anglesey Abbey, Cambridgeshire. The varied assemblage of works of art was brought together by the 1st Lord Fairhaven (1896–1966). Paintings include two superb Claudes, examples of the work of Cuyp, Gainsborough, Constable and Bonington; and over a hundred views of Windsor, one of the most complete topographical records of any historic site. – 18th c. furniture includes a *bureau à cylindre* by D. Roentgen, Sir Robert Walpole's mahogany writing desk from Houghton, and David Garrick's japanned dressing table. – Gobelins, Felletin, and Mortlake tapestries. – 16th and 17th c. bronzes. – Late medieval carved-wood statues; silver, ranging from a pair of vast 17th c. Dutch plaques to an imposing tray by Paul Storr and a famous targe modelled by Flaxman.

Ascott, Buckinghamshire. The nucleus of the collection, inherited from Leopold de Rothschild, came from Gunnersbury Park, but Anthony de Rothschild (1887–1961) built up the unusual display of Ming and K'ang Hsi wares. – Particularly strong in paintings of the Dutch 17th c. school, with Hobbema, Van Mieris, Maes, Jan Steen, de Jongh, the Ostades, Berchem, Wouverman, Van der Heyden, and not least Cuyp, all well represented; works of the English school are fewer, but of high quality (portraits by Gainsborough, Reynolds, Romney; a late Turner and a superb Stubbs); Italy contributes works by Andrea del Sarto, Lorenzo Lotto and G. B. Tiepolo. – French 18th c. furniture includes a black lacquer writing table bearing the stamps of Joseph Baumhauer and 'BVRB', and pieces signed by M. G. Cramer, Franz Rübestück, and the great J. H. Riesener; good English mid-Georgian furniture. – Isfahan carpets of the 16th and 17th c. – Famous oriental porcelain: Han, Sung and T'ang; but the glory of the collection is the display of wares combining relief decoration with turquoise, violet, aubergine and yellow glazes (these so-called *san ts'ai* [three colour] wares of the late Ming dynasty are outstanding in this country); numerous examples of the more familiar K'ang Hsi *famille verte, famille jaune* and *famille noire*.

Blickling, Norfolk. The Hobarts and their descendants lived at Blickling for over three hundred years; this is reflected in a long series of family portraits (many studio works, but original paintings by Mytens, Kneller, and Gainsborough). – Textiles include an early Exeter (?) carpet, a Moorfields carpet (*c.* 1770), Mortlake tapestries (*The Life of Abraham*), Flemish tapestries after Teniers, and a baroque tapestry depicting Peter the Great at Poltawa (presented by Catherine the Great to the 2nd Earl of Buckingham). – Apart from a Florentine 15th c. cassone, and one or two Continental 17th c. chests, most of the furniture is English and such as a visitor might expect to find in an imposing country house (the early 18th c. state bed came to Blickling as the perquisite of the 2nd Earl of Buckingham, Lord of the Bedchamber to George II). – The famous library, with no less than eighty incunabula, is composed largely of the collection formed by Sir Richard Ellys, Member of Parliament from 1719 to 1727; it reflects his interest in theology, philology and the classics, and contains a wealth of political pamphlets of the period.

Buscot Park, Oxfordshire. The collection was built by the 1st Lord Faringdon, and his successor. – Italian paintings of the 15th and 16th c.; the 17th c. contributes the outstanding work at Buscot, a portrait by Rembrandt (reputedly of his friend Clement de Jongh), and a Rubens, a Jourdaens and a Murillo; the English school is represented by Reynolds, Gainsborough, Wilson, Millais, Rossetti, Watts, Landseer, Leighton, Burne-Jones (a series of canvases illustrating *The Legend of the Briar Rose*), and Graham Sutherland. A small collection of drawings includes three studies by Rembrandt. – Elegant Neo-classical furniture: side tables designed by Robert Adam, others in the Sheraton style veneered in tortoiseshell, pieces in satinwood or rosewood with painted or inlaid decoration; and important examples of Thomas Hope's creations in the Egyptian manner. – Silver, porcelain, and minor works of art reflect discrimination and a catholic taste: Sung dishes, K'ang Hsi and Arita wares, 16th c. Urbino maiolica, Meissen, Derby, armorial *Compagnie des Indes*, and a lustre tea-service painted by Therese Lessor (Mrs W. R. Sickert); Renaissance ivories, oriental jade and cloisonné, blue john vases, and a mixed collection of bronzes.

Charlecote, Warwickshire. Sir Thomas Lucy, satirized by Shakespeare in the character of Justice Shallow, sat for his portrait to William Larkin; happily his descendants also proved inveterate sitters. Portraits by Kneller, Richardson, Batoni, Gainsborough, Raeburn and lesser artists. – The house (herein lies its special interest) was redecorated and refurnished in the 1820s and 1830s by George Lucy, with the guidance of Thomas Willement. Lucy had married an heiress in 1822 and bought extensively at the Fonthill sale in the following year (a great marble 16th c. table originally in the Borghese Palace, Gothick and Russian malachite tables, *pietra dura* and 19th c. boulle cabinets, small lacquer pieces, porcelain, and an ebony four-poster). The Drawing-Room today is a muted echo of Fonthill. – George Lucy, advised by William Pickering, the well-known early Victorian bookseller, also augmented the important library created by a bibliophile ancestor in the early 17th c. – Charlecote silver includes a rare Tudor silver-gilt wine-cup, and three 17th c. pieces, the gift of Charles II to a Bishop Lucy.

Clandon, Surrey. The contents represent a reasonably happy marriage between such Onslow pictures and furniture as remained in the house after its transfer to the Trust, and the Gubbay Collection bequeathed in 1969. – The legacy of the Onslows, a family distinguished since the mid-16th c., includes a likeness of the famous Speaker Onslow, a scene in the House of Commons by Thornhill and Hogarth, a number of Ferneleys, and six bird and animal paintings by Barlow. – The Onslows also acquired such characteristic country-house furnishings as a set of early Mortlake tapestries of *The Seasons* (*c.* 1640) and a set of Soho hunting panels woven about a century later, a state bed with hangings and chairs *en suite* of about 1700, side tables in the manner of William Kent, and a rococo mirror possibly by Matthias Lock. – Mrs Gubbay's bequest brought in fine oriental and European porcelain. These ceramics are distinguished for a flock of audacious Chinese birds, elegant Nymphenburg figures by Bustelli, and a Meissen 'monkey band' modelled by Kändler; the extensive collection of European china includes Bow, Chelsea, Derby, Sèvres, further Meissen porcelain, and a collection of early Staffordshire pottery. – The Gubbay Bequest includes a William and Mary table by Jensen, late 17th c. cabinets on gesso stands, early 18th c. pieces upholstered in contemporary needlework or tapestry, gesso tables by Gumley and Moore (*c.* 1725), an unusual green lacquer secretaire, and two George III commodes from the workshop of Pierre Langlois; mid-Georgian needlework carpets, and an Exeter carpet of about the same date.

1730s was to introduce Georgian furniture, the house retains its late Stuart contents and character. Unrivalled hangings, silk damasks, cut velvets and tapestries (a set of Flemish tapestries with designs after Poussin, an English series depicting *The Months*, and another series by Bradshaw of mid-18th c. date). – A wealth of 17th c. furniture, arranged by the Victoria and Albert Museum to accord wherever possible with an inventory of 1679 (lacquered and japanned pieces, marquetry, a set of gilded chairs carved with dolphins, and the famous silver 'chimney furniture'); many pieces have a distinctly Netherlandish flavour and Dutch craftsmen were no doubt employed. – Paintings (battle pieces, landscapes, seascapes) were also commissioned from Dutch artists, such as Van Wyck, Danckerts, Van de Velde and others. Historical and family portraits: no less than eight canvases by Lely hang in the Long Gallery, works by Vanderbank, Kneller and Reynolds; miniatures by Hilliard, Oliver and Cooper. Verrio and his studio were responsible for a number of painted ceilings.

Hardwick Hall, Derbyshire. Few interiors have survived with so little change, and Bess of Hardwick would recognize many of the objects listed in the 1601 inventory. The collection of 16th c. furniture, tapestries and embroideries is astonishingly rich. – No comparable body of Elizabethan embroidery survives elsewhere (sets of appliqué hangings depicting *The Virtues* and *The Liberal Arts*, panel of *The Judgment of Paris*, the renowned cushion-cover known as *Fancie of a Fowler*); a number of pieces are reasonably attributed to Mary Queen of Scots and her ladies. – The 16th c. tapestries are hardly less remarkable: such well-known Brussels or Flemish sets as *The Story of Ulysses, The Triumphs of Scipio, The Planets, The Story of Gideon* and *The Story of Abraham* (after designs by Van Orley), and a set of painted cloth hangings of the *Acts of the Apostles,* an example of a technique that has rarely survived; later tapestries include a Flemish set after designs by Jordaens, and panels of *Playing Boys* (Hatton Garden) after designs by Cleyn. – The 16th c. furniture is notable for a long walnut table inlaid with musical instruments and other devices (probably made for Bess of Hardwick's marriage in 1578), a square table inlaid with playing cards, two ebullient pieces derived from designs by Du Cerceau, a court cupboard in the more classical style associated with Jean Goujon, and a German inlaid chest of about 1570; later furniture includes a large set of 'farthingale' chairs and a state couch (both *c.* 1635), a set of elaborate gilt stools in the manner of Thomas Roberts, and two beds, one hung with early 17th c. embroidery and the other (*c.* 1700) with original Genoa velvet. – Cavendish family portraits.

Ickworth, Suffolk. The collection deriving from the Hervey family, and notably from that great dilettante the Earl–Bishop of Bristol, is chiefly remarkable for paintings, French furniture and silver. – Continental paintings include portraits by Titian and Velasquez, and a landscape by Gaspar Poussin; conversation pieces by Hogarth and Gravelot; seascapes by Dominic Serres; and West's much-reproduced *Death of Wolfe*. The Earl–Bishop himself was painted by Vigée le Brun, and the sequence of Hervey portraits lays under tribute Zoffany, Ramsay, Reynolds, Gainsborough (two portraits and a moving sketch), Romney, Hoppner and Lawrence. – The French furniture begins with a Louis XIV boulle writing table, and later pieces include a stamped Régence kingwood commode, a Louis XV *bureau de dame* by Roussel, a pair of gilt side tables of the same period with malachite tops (traditionally the gift of Catherine the Great to the 3rd Earl), a Louis XVI marquetry secretaire and a little parquetry table stamped P.H. – The splendid silver derives largely from the Earl–Bishop's predecessors who bought extensively from leading silversmiths, the 1st Earl showing a predilection for the elaborate confections of the Huguenot refugees: an imposing wine cistern (1680) by Robert Cooper; later pieces include tea caddies by Christian Hillan, wine coolers by Philip Rollos, tureens, baskets, casters and dishes by Lamerie or Kandler, twelve candelabra by Simon Le Sage, and many representative examples of the work of other craftsmen active between 1700 and 1760, such as Harache, Patel, Crespin and Pantin, The early 19th c. master, Paul Storr, is also well represented.

Lanhydrock, Cornwall. The Library, composed almost entirely of works published in the 16th and 17th c., is one of the most considerable in Trust ownership (15 incunabula; many books otherwise unrecorded in Britain; major collection of Civil War tracts). – Robartes family portraits (Dahl, Hudson, Romney, Richmond); Brussels and Mortlake tapestries; Louis XIV boulle writing tables, a fine George II upholstered suite, and good country-house pieces. – The Billiard Room, with its Victorian furnishings, is wonderfully evocative of the last century.

Knole, Kent. Since 1603 successive generations of Sackvilles have added to the treasures of the vast house. – The Jacobean and Carolean furniture, much of which has miraculously retained its original upholstery, is without parallel. The former comprises a group of X-framed chairs with their attendant stools (some deriving from the royal palaces at Hampton Court and Whitehall), a bed and furniture *en suite* with spangled appliqué decoration, a set of gilt chairs and settees with painted decoration, and the 'Knole Settee'. A Charles I billiard table, and a set of Cromwellian folding travelling chairs, lead on to the sumptuous display of Carolean sofas, chairs and stools in the Cartoon Gallery with Genoa velvets and tasselled fringes. Later Stuart taste is represented by the bed and carved giltwood furniture in the Venetian Ambassador's Room, attributed to Thomas Roberts, and the bed and matching furniture, silvered and gilded, in the King's Bedroom, both probably from Whitehall Palace. The famous silver furniture at Knole (fire dogs, sconces, table, dressing-set, tripod stands, and mirror) dates from 1662–85. – Textiles: an English 16th c. carpet, Persian carpets of the 16th and 17th c., sets of tapestries (notably a Flemish series depicting scenes from *Orlando Furioso, c.* 1600). – Pictures: The 3rd Duke of Dorset owned twenty-two paintings by his friend Reynolds and ten still hang at Knole; other works include portraits by Gainsborough, William Larkin (two), Mytens (three), Stretes, Van Dyck, Lely (three), Kneller (four), Dobson, Jervas and Hoppner.

Montacute, Somerset. The house was virtually empty when acquired by the Trust in 1931. It has been furnished from gifts and loans (notably the Malcolm Stewart bequest, and the extensive collection of Elizabethan and Jacobean paintings lent by the National Portrait Gallery). – Textiles: two Gothic 15th c. tapestries, a Gobelins from Neilson's *Nouvelles Indes* series, and the well-known early 18th c. needlework panels originally at Stoke Edith.

Nostell Priory, Yorkshire. Extensive collection of Chippendale furniture: some 100 pieces (ranging from elaborate commodes to a chopping block) are attributable to him, and in many cases the original bills survive. The furniture is representative both of his earlier *Director* style (e.g. a highly rococo set of ribbon-back chairs) and of his Neo-classical work, of which there are numerous examples executed to Robert Adam's designs. The State Bedchamber and Dressing-Room, for which Chippendale supplied even the Chinese wallpaper, show him also as a master of lacquer furniture. – Pictures include a full-size contemporary copy of Holbein's portrait of *Sir Thomas More and His Family*, and a representative collection of English and Continental works. – Tapestries from *The Four Continents* series by Van der Borcht, *c.* 1750.

Osterley Park, Middlesex. An unrivalled display of Neo-classical furniture, mainly of the 1770s, designed by Robert Adam and John Linnell. Though the original collection of pictures has gone (works by Reynolds, Cotes, Wilson and others are on loan), the furniture in the state rooms (candlestands, candelabra, mirrors, commodes, desks and seat furniture) has survived. Recorded room by room in an inventory of 1782, it has been arranged by the Victoria and Albert Museum in the formal fashion of the time. Among distinguished pieces are a state bed, one of Adam's most ambitious designs; the Drawing-Room commodes, veneered in hardwood; John Linnell's mahogany furniture in the Library; painted 'Etruscan' pieces; and upholstered chairs and settees in the Tapestry Room which, like the wall hangings, incorporate designs by Boucher.

Penrhyn Castle, Gwynedd. Thomas Hopper (1776–1856), who designed the Neo-Norman castle, was also entrusted with the design and choice of furniture. The outcome was highly unusual. Much of the furniture, even to the *tables de nuit* in the bedrooms, is uncompromisingly 'Norman', as Hopper conceived the style. A number of pieces are in slate, among them a forbidding four-poster bed (the Penrhyn family derived their wealth from adjacent slate quarries). – Paintings from the collection assembled in the 19th c. by the 1st Lord Penrhyn. – Exhibition of some 800 dolls from all over the world, many of them dating from the 17th and 18th c.; museum of industrial locomotives in the stables.

Petworth, Sussex. A varied assemblage of works of art reflects the taste and wealth of successive generations of Percys, Seymours and Wyndhams. – The pictures are outstanding. An imposing series by Van Dyck and Lely were bought in the 17th c.; the set of 'Petworth Beauties' by Dahl, and a magic Claude of *Jacob and Laban*, followed soon after; in the first half of the 18th c. the 2nd Earl of Egremont introduced works by Ruisdael, Van Goyen, Van der Meulen, Bourdon and Snyders; the 3rd Earl of Egremont, an enlightened patron of contemporary English painting, further enlarged the collection, endowing Petworth with three Gainsboroughs, three Wilsons, three Blakes, a dozen Reynolds, no less than twenty Turners, and numerous works by lesser artists, such as Thomas Philipps, Wilkie and Fuseli. There are also a version of *The Epiphany* by Bosch, a set of eight small religious scenes by Elsheimer, a romantic early portrait by Titian, and works by Le Nain, Bellotto, Cuyp and Hobbema. – The 3rd Earl was also a patron of contemporary sculpture (Carew, Flaxman, Rossi, Westmacott) which he installed, together with some fifty classical marbles (mainly Hellenistic or late Roman) collected by the 2nd Earl, in one of the few 18th c. sculpture galleries to survive. – Fine furniture; Chelsea, Meissen, and oriental porcelain; 17th and 18th c. silver and pieces by Paul Storr (notably a set of twelve wine-coolers).

Polesden Lacey, Surrey. Three groups of important paintings: Dutch 17th c. masters (the Ostades, Cuyp, Van der Neer, Van der Velde, de Hoogh, Van Goyen, Salomon van Ruysdael, Van der Heyden, Teniers, Jacob Ruisdael and Ter Borch) mainly acquired in the 1890s; English portraits (Richardson, Reynolds, Lawrence, and four Raeburns) bought for the most part soon after the First World War; Italian and Flemish paintings of the 14th to 16th c. (including works by Luca di Tommé, Perugino, the Master of St Severin and Bernard van Orley) which reflect the taste of the 1930s. – The French furniture ranges in period from a Renaissance table in the manner of Jacques du Cerceau (*c.* 1570) to gilt settees in the elaborate style of Georges Jacob (d. 1814); walnut set of Régence seat furniture (*c.* 1730) with contemporary needlework covers; Louis XV and XVI commodes, bureaux and *tables ambulantes*, include a number of signed pieces (Tuart, Boudin, Genty, Carel, Jean Demoulin). — Ceramics: Urbino ware of the 16th c.; remarkable pieces of the K'ang Hsi period, both 'powder blue' and *famille verte*; *famille rose* of the later Ch'ien Lung period is also well represented; outstanding European porcelain from Germany (Meissen, Fürstenberg and Nymphenburg). — English silver: 17th c. tankards, tazze, and two-handled porringers (many pieces dating from the 1680s are decorated with Chinoiserie figures, birds and foliage).

Powis Castle, Powys. The castle was already 300 years old when it came into the ownership of the Herberts in 1587, and successive generations have left their imprint on the collection. Family portraits span four hundred years, (works by Reynolds, Gainsborough, Romney and Nathaniel Dance); Mortlake and Brussels tapestries (one set signed by Marcus de Vos); good 18th c. furniture, notably a set of Queen Anne chairs and settee upholstered in their original Spitalfields velvet, and a pair of black lacquer commodes of about 1765 attributed to Pierre Langlois. — Powis is full of surprises: Greek red-figure vases of the 4th c. B.C., the state sword of the Lord of the Marches (*c.* 1500), 16th c. Limoges enamels, a monumental Italian 16th c. table inlaid with marbles and semi-precious stones, a view of Verona by Bellotto, and an exotic collection formed in India by the 1st Lord Clive.

Saltram, Devon. The collection owes almost everything to John Parker, who succeeded in 1768. He added to earlier family portraits no less than ten paintings by his friend Reynolds, nine by Gilbert Stuart and seven by Angelica Kaufmann. He probably also acquired most of the Italian paintings, including a rare altarpiece by Samacchini (?), and works by Dutch and Flemish masters (Neefs, De Hoogh, Rubens). Much of the interest of these paintings derives from the fact that the collection was virtually complete by 1820 and that little has come in since. — John Parker also engaged the services of Adam and Chippendale, who were severally responsible for designing and making much of the furniture (mahogany card tables, giltwood seat furniture and no doubt the *torchères* that carry Boulton's sumptuous candelabra in blue john and tortoiseshell mounted in ormolu). Other pieces include a large Louis XIV boulle writing table, and a marquetry writing desk of the same period by the rare *ébéniste* M.-B. Evalde. — Pottery and porcelain was also bought by John Parker: a large collection of Wedgwood vases; local Plymouth pieces; imposing services of Worcester and Marseilles (the latter with the Parker crest); and oriental 18th c. export wares.

Shugborough, Staffordshire. Objects in the house since the 18th c. include Anson portraits (Hudson, Reynolds), a highly elaborate Chinese Chippendale display cabinet, Chinese mirror paintings, and a Chinese export armorial service. But most of the contents were sold in 1842, and the existing collection largely represents the taste and acquisitions of the 2nd Earl of Lichfield, after 1850. – Much 18th c. French furniture, with signed pieces by Bury, Riesener, Delaitre, Schmitz and Rübestuck; dining-room side tables (c. 1735), attributed to Matthias Lock. – 18th c. silver by Lamerie, Sieber, Wakelin, Romer, Flaxman, and others. – There are numerous watercolour drawings of Sudbury by Moses Griffith and by Nicholas Dall (who was also responsible for the inset paintings in the Dining-Room), and a collection of 19th c. sporting pictures mainly by William Webb and Thomas Weaver, with Landseer contributing a number of animal studies.

Stourhead, Wiltshire. 18th and early 19th c. furniture, much of it supplied by Giles Grendey in the 1740s and by the Younger Chippendale between 1795 and 1820. The latter was responsible for the complete furnishing of the Library and Picture Gallery. – Paintings, mainly collected by Henry Hoare (d. 1785) and Sir Richard Colt Hoare (d. 1838), include works by Nicolas and Gaspar Poussin, Vernet, Orizonte, Maratta, Mengs, Cigoli, Zuccarelli, Angelica Kaufmann and Cotes, and a series of topographical views by the Swiss watercolourist Louis Ducros. – Sculptures by Le Sueur, Rysbrack, Cheere and Lucas.

Sudbury, Derbyshire. Paintings: murals by Laguerre; Griffier's view of Sudbury (c. 1680); several portraits by J. M. Wright (including a likeness of George Vernon, the builder of the house); works by Soest, Dahl, Kneller, Enoch Seeman, Vanderbank, Hudson, Hoppner and Lawrence. – 17th and 18th c. furniture, notably a Flemish early 17th c. cabinet with painted panels by Frans Francken, late 17th c. console tables, and good lacquer. – Greek and Etruscan vases, Liverpool delftware (c. 1770), and oriental export china.

Tatton Park, Cheshire. The Entrance Hall at once strikes the note of eclectic connoisseurship that characterizes the house: Italian Renaissance chests, a Florentine cassone, Goanese cabinet, and 18th c. Japanese dishes. – The early 19th c. furniture is of the first importance: rosewood and ebony, inlaid with brass and pewter, supplied by Le Gaigneur, and a quantity of furniture by Gillow of Lancaster. Much of the Gillow furniture, which includes a satinwood bookcase with ebony inlay, is minutely documented, and ranges from Neo-Grecian austerity to the full-blown Continental taste of c. 1825. Gillow provided all the Library furniture, and also furnished the bedrooms (1811–12). – There are portraits by Hans Eworth, Pourbus, Nazzari, Gardner, Lawrence and Beechey; landscapes, religious and genre paintings by Van Dyck, Guercino,

Rosa, Van der Neer, De Heem, and Berchem. — Silvergilt by Hennel, Storr and Benjamin Smith. — Delft ware, Chelsea, Worcester and Minton porcelain.

Treasurer's House, York. The furniture collected by Frank Green (d. 1930) is of high quality; four pieces are illustrated in Edwards's *Dictionary of Furniture* and half a dozen receive mention in Macquoid's volumes. — 17th c. oak, much gilt gesso, late Stuart *verre eglomisé* mirrors, Queen Anne walnut secretaire bookcase, early 18th c. giltwood chandeliers, two George II beds (probably from Houghton Hall), a set of mahogany chairs (*c.* 1765), attributed to Robert Mainwaring, Régence parcelgilt consoles, and Louis XIV boulle writing table veneered in brass and tortoiseshell with designs in the manner of Berain. — Collection of 18th c. glass; 17th c. Delft and 18th c. Stafford and Yorkshire ware.

Uppark, Sussex. In its extraordinary state of preservation, the famous doll's-house, with its Queen Anne furniture, hall-marked silver, Waterford glass, seems like a microcosm of Uppark itself. The doll's-house belonged to the lady whom Sir Matthew Fetherstonhaugh married in 1747. Shortly afterwards the couple laid their imprint firmly on Uppark, acquiring most of the interesting pictures and the wealth of mid-18th c. furniture, much of it reflecting Chippendale's *Director* style. — Furniture: among their purchases are a pair of carved and parcel-gilt rococo side tables with Florentine scagliola tops (dated 1754), a gilt drawing-room suite upholstered with Soho tapestry of about the same date, a set of chairs in the style of Robert Mainwaring (*c.* 1765), and a pair of English lacquered commodes in the French taste, with enrichments in carved wood instead of ormolu, made some five years later. A large Louis XV boulle writing table and four boulle pedestals by the *ébéniste* Levasseur may have been introduced by their son, Sir Harry. — Paintings: Sir Matthew and his wife when in Italy acquired six Luca Giordanos that illustrate the parable of *The Prodigal Son*, four competent views of Venice (Canaletto studio), six Vernet landscapes, and not least eight early portraits by Batoni; a number of characteristic small paintings by Devis represent Sir Matthew's wife's family; other works by Tillemans (early views of Uppark), Swanveldt, Snyders and Zuccarelli. — Porcelain: Sèvres, and a Ch'ien Lung armorial service.

Upton House, Warwickshire. The 2nd Lord Bearsted (d. 1948) was a discriminating and dedicated collector. Pictures and porcelain at Upton reflect his exacting standards. — Acquired mainly after 1920, there are some 150 paintings. The Gallery is devoted to works of the 15th and 16th c., and primarily to masters of the Italian Renaissance and their Flemish and French contemporaries. Flemish and German works: a grisaille by Peter Brueghel the Elder depicting *The Dormition of the Virgin*, religious subjects by the 15th c. Master of the St Lucy Legend and Jan Provoost, *Madonna and Child* by Gerard David, triptych of *The Adoration of the Magi* by Hieronymus Bosch, *St George and the Dragon* attributed to Michael Pacher, and three small but excellent portraits by Roger van der Weyden, Memling and Holbein. Italian works: *Presentation of the Virgin* by Giovanni di Paolo, *Last Supper* in the style of Giotto, *Two Apostles* by Carlo Crivelli. French works: two unknown sitters in the style of Corneille de Lyon, jewel-like portraits of François I and Henri II from Clouet's studio, and a series of 15th c. miniatures illustrating *The Story of Melusine*. In the Passage Gallery are hung a 15th c. miniature by Fouquet, El Greco's *El Espolio*, three paintings of Venice and a drawing which show Guardi at the height of his powers, two works attributed to Rembrandt, a Tintoretto and a Lotto, and characteristic examples of the work of Jan Steen, Metsu, Van der Heyden and Jacob Ruisdael. The English school is well represented elsewhere in the house: three masterpieces by Stubbs, Hogarth's *Morning* and *Evening*, sporting scenes by Marshall and Sartorius, portraits by Devis, Zoffany, Reynolds, Raeburn and Romney. – The Bearsted porcelain is particularly strong in the soft paste of Sèvres and Chelsea. The Sèvres pieces made to the royal order of Catherine the Great and Louis XVI offer special interest, and the English porcelain is notable for a few rare figures of the red anchor period, and an unrivalled collection of figures of the gold anchor period, including Apollo and the Nine Muses.

The Vyne, Hampshire. John Chute, dilettante and friend of Horace Walpole, collected most of the interesting furniture. Much of it is documented and can be traced in 18th c. inventories: e.g. Charles II stools and cabinets, William and Mary walnut secretaire, set of twelve Queen Anne walnut chairs, Chinese Chippendale mahogany side tables of 1765, pair of commodes in the French taste of about the same date, rococo side tables with green marble tops related to designs by Batty Langley. There are bills for a large suite of seat furniture from Bradbourn and France, and for chairs, leather-covered benches and not least a richly carved gilt stand for an Italian *pietra dura* casket (1752) from Vile and Cobb. A table in the style of Kent with an elaborate scagliola top came from Strawberry Hill (possibly as a gift from Horace Walpole). – Paintings on the whole are undistinguished, but there are works by Oudry, Rosalba, and a group by J. H. Muntz (a protégé of John Chute). – Soho tapestries woven by Vanderbank (*c.* 1720); Nymphenburg and Meissen figures; Italian maiolica (*c.* 1730); a set of painted glass plates bought by Chute in Venice. – Interesting sculpture: 16th c. terracotta head of the Emperor Probus, four Italian baroque busts of emperors once owned by Godoy, chief minister to Charles IV of Spain, and a recumbent effigy of Challoner Chute by Carter. – The chapel contains Flemish 16th c. stained glass of unmatched brilliance and clarity.

Waddesdon Manor, Buckinghamshire. When the published Waddesdon catalogue is complete it will run to something like twenty folio volumes. In a brief compass it is impossible to do more than indicate the richness of the vast collection built up by Baron Ferdinand de Rothschild and other members of the family. The collection has a marked French flavour, and is rightly renowned for the superb assembly of French works of art of the late 17th and 18th c.: marquetry furniture, sculptures, paintings, Sèvres, gold boxes and Savonnerie carpets. – French paintings: Watteau, and his followers Lancret and Pater, contribute no less than eleven works, Boucher six and Greuze four; earlier portraits in the manner of Clouet and Corneille de Lyon. Dutch and Flemish works include Rubens's *Garden of Love*, four Cuyps, three Van der Heydens, De Hoogh, Van Orley, Ter Borch, Dou, and Jacob van Ruisdael. Venetian painting is represented by Guardi (two enormous views of *The Basin of St Mark's*, six studies of the Venetian islands, and four small portrait panels). British painting: ten dazzling portraits by Reynolds (*Captain St Leger*, '*Perdita*'), seven by Gainsborough (*The Pink Boy* and another likeness of '*Perdita*'), and three by Romney. – French 18th c. furniture, comprising well over a hundred pieces, includes signed works by most of the better known *ébénistes* (Dubois, Genty, Roussel, Baumhauer, Montigny, Cressent, a dozen by the incomparable Riesener, and several mounted with Sèvres plaques by Carlin). Also innumerable clocks, candelabra, wall lights. – Fabrics: a unique series of Savonnerie carpets, many of them made for Versailles; Gobelins, Aubusson, Beauvais (*La Noble Pastorale* after designs by Boucher) tapestries. – Sculptures: notably by Clodion, Falconet, and Pajou. – Porcelain and pottery: famous collection of Sèvres (*vaisseaux à mât*, wine-coolers, pot pourri vases, jardinières, inkstands, a vast 'bleu celeste' dinner service; many pieces painted by such well-known decorators as Morin and Dodin); Meissen (series of figures by Kändler); Deruta, Urbino, Castel Durante and Faenza maiolica; Chinese celadon wares sumptuously mounted in ormolu. – Collections of gold boxes (many painted with miniature landscapes by Van Blarenberghe); Renaissance works of art; 16th and 17th c. arms and armour; books (mosaic and armorial bindings).

Wallington, Northumberland. A varied collection that spans two and a half centuries and reflects in particular the wide interests of the Trevelyan family. – The furniture (Gothick Chippendale, Régence commodes) is good but not exceptional; it includes a number of Dutch 18th c. marquetry pieces probably introduced in the 1880s. – By contrast the collection of pottery and porcelain is outstanding: Chinese and Japanese export wares; early Italian maiolica; English delft; rare Bow figures and Derby partridge tureens; Meissen, including a set of *Continents* (*c.* 1745) modelled by Kändler; Sèvres, Vienna, etc. – English paintings include a Reynolds, a Gainsborough (? partially repainted by Reynolds), and among later works eight large canvases depicting scenes from Northumbrian history by W. B. Scott. – Silver by Kandler, Jacobs and other

18th c. craftsmen; a highly important set of needlework panels (*c.* 1725); Lord Macaulay's library.

West Wycombe Park, Buckinghamshire. Sir Francis Dashwood, who re-modelled the house and reigned at West Wycombe for over half a century, was responsible for collecting most of the furniture, pictures and sculpture. – Furniture: a few pieces date from before Sir Francis's time (e.g. an unusual triple mirror with *verre eglomisé* borders, an Italian 17th c. cabinet inlaid with lapis and semi-precious stones, and a pair of lacquer cabinets of about 1700), but in general the furniture is a striking expression of mid-18th c. taste, with such things as rococo mirrors and side tables in the Chippendale *Director* manner. Perhaps the most significant pieces are four marquetry commodes almost certainly by Pierre Langlois. – Paintings: with the exception of four landscapes by Orizonte, Sir Francis's 'Grand Tour' paintings are not of great quality, but they illustrate the marked preference for Italian baroque charac-teristic of many 18th c. dilettanti; there are works also by Lely, Jacob van Ruisdael, and one of the only known likenesses of Milton; and ceilings painted by Guiseppe and Giovanni Borgnis. – Sculpture: classical marbles and plaster busts of emperors are indicative of Sir Francis's love of all things Roman; there are also busts of literary worthies (probably by John Cheere), and marbles of *The Seasons* by Delvaux (1770). – Tapestries: a Mortlake pair from *The Months* after Van Orley (1670), and a Brussels set of *Peasant Scenes* woven by De Vos after designs by Teniers.

Wightwick Manor, Staffordshire. The only Trust house with a considerable Pre-Raphaelite collection. – Morris fabrics and papers, De Morgan tiles, stained glass by Kempe, furniture by Bodley and Voysey, Kelmscott Press publications. – Paintings and drawings by prominent members of the Brother-hood and their friends include works by Brett, Ford Madox Brown, Burne-Jones, Holman Hunt, Leighton, Millais, May Morris, Rossetti, Ruskin and Watts.

Index

Bold figures denote plate numbers